The Empress :

Napoleon's Enchantress

(Volume I)

Philip W. Sergeant

Alpha Editions

This edition published in 2019

ISBN : 9789353977115

Design and Setting By
Alpha Editions
email - alphaedis@gmail.com

THE
EMPRESS JOSEPHINE

NAPOLEON'S ENCHANTRESS

By
PHILIP W. SERGEANT

Author of " The Last Empress of the French," etc

WITH 34 ILLUSTRATIONS

Vol. I

New York
DODD, MEAD & CO.

372 FIFTH AVENUE
1909

CONTENTS

VOL. I

ILLUSTRATIONS

VOL. I

vii

THE EMPRESS JOSEPHINE

CHAPTER I

JOSEPHINE'S FAMILY

WRITING in 1887, after a trip to Fort-de-France, formerly Fort-Royal, capital of the West Indian island of Martinique, the late Lafcadio Hearn remarks that the town has little of outward interest apart from the Savane, the great green public square. But that, continues Hearn in his most enthusiastic strain, would be worth the visit alone, even were it not made romantic by the marble memory of Josephine:

" I went to look at the white dream of her there, a creation of master-sculptors. It seemed to me absolutely lovely. Sea-winds have bitten it ; tropical rains have streaked it ; some microscopic growth has darkened the exquisite hollow of the throat. And yet such is the human charm of the figure that you almost fancy you are gazing at a living presence. Perhaps the profile is less artistically real—statuesque to the point of betraying the chisel ; but when you look straight up into the sweet Creole face, you can believe she lives : all the wonderful West Indian charm of the woman is there. She is standing just in front of the Savane, robed in the fashion of the First Empire, with gracious arms and shoulders bare : one hand leans upon a medallion bearing the eagle profile of Napoleon. Seven tall palms stand in a circle around her, lifting their comely heads into the blue glory of the tropic day. Within their enchanted circle you feel that you tread holy ground—the sacred soil of artist and poet. Here the recollections of memoir-writers vanish away ; the gossip of history is hushed for you ; you no longer care to know how rumour has it that she spoke or smiled or wept : only the bewitchment of her lives under the thin, soft, swaying shadows of those feminine palms. Over the violet space of summer sea, through the vast splendour of azure light, she is looking back to the place of her birth, back to beautiful drowsy

Trois-Ilets—and always with the same half-dreaming, half-plaintive smile—unutterably touching." [1]

It would surely be impossible to find any passage in literature outside these few lines from the early pen of Lafcadio Hearn in which a better suggestion is conveyed to us of the Josephine of romance, as opposed to the Josephine of history. And the Josephine of romance may be said to bear to the actual Josephine as we find her in history the same relation that the statue so lovingly described above bore to the real woman, the wife of the First Consul and the Emperor, who never appeared without her rouge and thick coating of powder, who spent at least three hours in her dressing-room every morning, and who felt so keenly the necessity, if not of suffering, at any rate of labouring hard, to be beautiful. Yet it may be that, just as the living woman was able to exercise upon those with whom she came in contact a fascination which no statue of her could inspire, so there is more absorbing interest in the true Josephine, seen as she existed from

[1] Lafcadio Hearn, "Two Years in the French West Indies," pp. 65–6.

day to day, with her frivolity and her faults so
little hidden, than in the merely lovely and
benevolent Empress of legend. Whatever legend
could do for the first wife of Napoleon Bonaparte,
it could not invent for her a more curiously
picturesque career than was hers in fact : on the
contrary, in removing from its records so many
of the actual incidents as not harmonising with
the character which it was endeavouring to
present, it removed also a great deal of the
picturesqueness.

On June 23, 1763, there was born at Trois-
Ilets, Martinique, the eldest child of Joseph-
Gaspard Tascher de la Pagerie, retired lieutenant of marine artillery, and of his wife,
formerly Rose-Claire des Vergers de Sannois.
To this child were given the names of Marie-
Joseph-Rose ; Marie from her father's mother,
Joseph from her father, and Rose from her
mother. The name of Josephine was unknown
until she met the young General Bonaparte in
1796. In her girlhood, up to the time when she
first sailed for France, she was generally called
by the pet-name of Yeyette, which sounds like an
infantile mispronunciation or a negro corruption.

At the time of Yeyette's birth her father and mother were both under thirty years of age and had been married a year and a half. Joseph-Gaspard Tascher de la Pagerie was one of the five children of a Frenchman who had emigrated to the West Indies in 1726. The Taschers were a family of provincial nobility in the Orléanais district of France. Although claiming to trace themselves back in history to the twelfth century, they had achieved nothing to raise them from a modest station in life. The estate of La Pagerie was in the neighbourhood of Blois, and the eldest branch of the family took the name of Tascher de la Pagerie (or Lapagerie, as it was often written) after establishing itself there. Gaspard-Joseph, though the eldest son of his father, went to the West Indies with little in his pocket and without official rank, from which it has been suggested that he was a ne'er-do-well. Those whose political views made them hostile to the Empress Josephine's family pictured its founder as picking up a bare living in the service of various Martinique households. All that is certain is that his emigration to the New World did not make his fortune. His best stroke was his marriage, eight years after he reached Martinique, to a Mlle. de la Chevalerie, with whom he received as dowry some property at Carbet, near Saint-Pierre, and some also in the island of Saint-Lucia. His debts accumulated, however, and he left his Carbet estate, where his son Joseph-Gaspard was born, and went to live at Fort-Royal. At the age of seventeen Joseph-Gaspard was sent to France as a rather elderly page in the household of the Dauphine, returning to Martinique three years later with the brevet rank of sub-lieutenant of marine artillery. This was the year in which warfare broke out between France and England in American waters ; and French needs in the West Indies brought about an appointment which had momentous consequences for the family of Tascher de la Pagerie.

In the spring of 1757 the home of the Taschers at Fort-Royal was inhabited by the father and mother, with their son Joseph-Gaspard and their three daughters, Marie-Euphémie-Désirée, Marie-Paule, and Marie-Françoise-Rose, aged twenty-one, nineteen, and seventeen respectively. Another son, Robert-Marguerite, was in France. None of the children were married, and the family was in poor circumstances, although the father had succeeded in persuading the Martinique authorities to register his letters of nobility, which entitled him to certain reliefs and privileges. The advent of the specially appointed Governor and Lieutenant-General of the Antilles was doubtless looked forward to with hope ; and Gaspard-Joseph Tascher was successful in getting for his eldest daughter an appointment as companion of some sort to the Governor's wife.

Messire François de Beauharnais, *haut et puissant seigneur*, as he was styled in the Royal appointment under which he came out to the French West Indian possessions, was a wealthy man of forty-two years of age when he arrived at Martinique with his young wife and his one-year-old child, named, like himself, François. His family, like that of the Taschers, came from the Orléanais (which may account for Marie-Euphémie-Désirée obtaining her post at Government House), but it had prospered better than the Taschers, owing to the military achievements of several past Beauharnais. His conduct while Governor shows him to have been a weak and unprincipled man ; but he was possessed

of considerable influence at Court, as is proved
by the manner in which he managed to escape
much of the punishment due to his misdeeds,
and even to secure a pension for his supposed
services.

Before the arrival of Beauharnais, Joseph-
Gaspard Tascher had gained the substantive
rank of lieutenant for the share which he had
taken in protecting Fort-Royal against English
attacks. It was not, however, the military
abilities of Josephine's future father, but the
talents of his sister that were to bring about
the close connection between the Taschers and
Beauharnais. Marie-Euphémie-Désirée Tascher
was a remarkable woman, as will clearly appear
from her subsequent history, and as strong a
character as François de Beauharnais was weak.
Her entry into Government House at Fort-
Royal decided the future lives of many persons.
She rapidly gained a complete ascendancy over
the Governor, while impressing his wife so
favourably that she remained on terms of friendship with her for at least four years, in spite of
the talk to which the intimacy of Beauharnais
and the Creole girl inevitably gave rise. Perhaps it was with a desire to disarm suspicion

that the Governor endeavoured to arrange a marriage for Marie-Euphémie-Désirée with a young man on his personal staff, Alexis Renaudin, who belonged to one of the best Martinique families. Renaudin's parents, however, objected to the match, both on account of the Taschers' poor position and because the lady, they said, abused her influence with M. and Mme. de Beauharnais. Consequently it was not until the father of Alexis died that the Governor was able to bring about the marriage. The widow yielded to pressure, and the wedding was celebrated on April 22, 1759.

It was owing to his fatherly exertions on behalf of his wife's companion that Beauharnais lost his post in the West Indies. The English fleet had attacked the island of Guadeloupe in January, and Beauharnais had received sufficient reinforcements to go to the aid of the French garrison early in March. Delaying six weeks in order to assist at the Renaudin marriage, he arrived at Guadeloupe in time to learn that Nadau du Treil, who was in command on the island, had surrendered a day previously. The rumour was spread about that the delay had been caused by the wedding

at Saint-Pierre of the Governor's son. In
reality, of course, this son was only three years
old, and the wedding which lost Guadeloupe
was that of Renaudin and Mlle. Tascher.
Beauharnais, however, paid for his neglect of
duty. Although he was able to put the blame
for the surrender of Guadeloupe upon Nadau
du Treil and his fellow officers, who were court-
martialled, degraded, and sent home to prison,
information as to the Governor's share in the
island's loss, if not as to its actual cause,
reached Paris, and in spite of his influence at
Court he was relieved of his command in the
West Indies.

Beauharnais did not return home at once.
His wife was expecting her second child, which
furnished a reasonable pretext for delay. On
May 26, 1760, she gave birth to her son Alex-
andre-François-Marie, afterwards first husband
of Josephine. The infant's *ondoiement*, though
not his full baptism, took place on June 10 at
Saint-Pierre, his godmother being Mme. Renaudin. On the same day the latter sailed
for France, according to the local tradition
accepted by Aubenas, whom we may call the
official biographer of Josephine. M. Masson,

who is less concerned than Aubenas to demon-
strate the virtuous character of Mme. Renaudin,
points out the lack of evidence of her presence
in Paris before 1761. In the April of that
year Beauharnais, with his wife and elder
child, sailed from Martinique on the frigate
Hébé. It is not a matter of very much importance whether Mme. Renaudin went with
them. It is certain that since her marriage
she had wielded more influence than ever
over the Beauharnais, and her relations with
her husband were strained to breaking-
point. She never lived with Renaudin again
after leaving Martinique, although there
does not appear to have been any legal
separation.

When the Beauharnais set sail for France,
they left the infant Alexandre with his grandmother at Fort-Royal. Seven months later,
on November 9, 1761, the marriage took place
at Trois-Ilets of the parents of Alexandre's
future wife. The Beauharnais influence was
seemingly advantageous to Joseph-Gaspard
Tascher as well as to his sister ; for his bride
belonged to the des Vergers de Sannois, one
of the best island families, and brought him

some much-needed relief, the dowry including
an estate at Trois-Ilets, where he made his
home with his wife and her father and mother,
and where he was living at the time of his eldest
daughter's birth.

French writers, whether friendly or not to
the Empress Josephine, have been careful to
insist on the fact that she was a Frenchwoman
by birth, although narrowly escaping being
born when Martinique was in the possession
of England. The island had been surrendered
by Beauharnais's successor, Levassor de la
Touche, among those captured with the new
Governor being Joseph-Gaspard Tascher, who
was said to have distinguished himself by holding
out for nine hours against the English attack
on the battery under his command. But in
March 1763, news of the Treaty of Paris reached
the West Indies, and early in June the French
fleet commissioned to take back the lost possessions reached the islands. Martinique was
therefore once again French property when
Madame Joseph-Gaspard Tascher gave birth
to her daughter, baptised five weeks later
under the names of Marie-Joseph-Rose.

It may be noted here that the doubt which

was at one time thrown on the date of Josephine's birth arose chiefly from the fact that she herself made a false declaration at the time of her marriage with Napoleon Bonaparte, when she stated her birthday to be June 23, 1767. In the "Mémorial de Sainte-Hélène" the statement that Josephine "deceived her husband by five or six years at least and produced the baptismal certificate of a younger sister, long since dead," is incorrect. Josephine's "deceit" was to the extent of four years only, and Napoleon connived at it, adding eighteen months to his own age, so as to make Josephine and himself almost the same in years. Further, the date of June 23, 1767, was not the birthday of either of the two younger Tascher sisters. They were born at Trois-Ilets in the course of the three following years—Catherine-Désirée on December 11, 1764, and Marie-Françoise on September 3, 1766.

If Josephine herself was responsible for one confusion about the date of her birth, she was in no way to blame for other doubts cast upon it. Had these doubts been justified, she would have been actually little more than a year older than she represented herself to be in

March 1796. Researchers discovered in Martinique two documents which appeared to make the Empress Josephine none other than Marie-Françoise, youngest daughter of Joseph-Gaspard Tascher and his wife. A registration was found of the death of Catherine-Désirée on October 16, 1777, and also a certificate of the burial of " Marie-Joseph-Rose " on November 5, 1791. The death of the second daughter was never in dispute. But why was the daughter who died in 1791 buried in her sister's name, if she was not actually the girl born in 1763 ? M. Masson hazards an ingenious conjecture, which may be true, though there is no evidence to support it. He mentions a document, of doubtful authenticity, which recorded the birth of a female child to a Demoiselle de Tascher on March 17, 1786 (when Josephine was in France), and suggests that Marie-Françoise, to shield herself, may have given her married sister's names instead of her own in the baptismal certificate, and that these names were retained in her burial certificate five years later.

In connection with this illegitimate child of a Demoiselle de Tascher, it is rather strange that the enemies of Josephine did not seize on the fact that Decrès, writing by Napoleon's order in 1807, spoke of "the demoiselle of eighteen years, whom Madame de la Pagerie has taken in and adopted." Had this girl, Marie-Bénaquette Tascher de la Pagerie, been really only eighteen years of age, she must have been born about 1789, that is to say, when Josephine was at Trois-Ilets during a two years' stay with her family, after her rupture with Alexandre de Beauharnais. Therefore on the ground of date alone there would have been no reason why Josephine, and not Marie-Françoise, should not have been the mother.

CHAPTER II

THE early part of Josephine's life has no place in history, for the reason that it was never chronicled ; and this was the case because there was nothing in it which seemed worth chronicling until thirty years later. She herself kept no records of her childish days, and those writers who claimed to give any description of them drew entirely on their imagination. Aubenas alone had access to the archives of the Tascher de la Pagerie family, and on his selection from the letters and documents which he was allowed to see depends what knowledge we have of the first fifteen years of our heroine's existence. And hardly before she is fourteen do we begin to get any personal details even from the biography of Aubenas.

Not long after the birth of his eldest daughter, Joseph-Gaspard Tascher was fortunate enough to receive from the French Government, as a reward for his services in the defence of Martinique against the English, a pension of four hundred and fifty livres a year. Doubtless the Beauharnais influence at Court helped to secure this grant, which was small in comparison with the pension of twelve thousand livres and the title of marquis which François de Beauharnais obtained for himself in spite of his achievement at Guadeloupe. The yearly four hundred and fifty saved Tascher from complete ruin ; for in August 1766 a great tempest, combined with earthquake, devastated Martinique, throwing down houses all over the island and wrecking plantations, while the sea overflowed the coasts and completed the damage. On the Taschers' estate nothing was left standing except the sugar-refinery, to which the owner with his wife and two infant children fled for shelter on August 13. In this building, altered so as to make it habitable, the family continued to live for the next twenty-five years ; and it was here that Josephine spent her life between the ages of three and ten.

The small town of Trois-Ilets lies on the opposite side to Fort-Royal of the bay now

known as that of Fort-de-France, and takes
its name from three little islands rising out
of the sea in front of it. Aubenas visited
the place in the middle of last century, when
it was not very much changed since the days
of Josephine's childhood. The town of Trois-
Ilets then contained about fifty wooden houses
and a modest church, in which was the family
vault of the Taschers. The Three Islets had
only a few fishermen's huts upon them, about
which spread the nets drying in the sun. To
reach the estate it was necessary to keep the
town on one's left hand, and it took about a
quarter of an hour's walk to reach a high point
on the road whence the old buildings could be
seen. The detailed description of Aubenas is
worth quotation :

" Situated on a small eminence surrounded
by larger hills, once covered by rich plantations
and now for the most part given up to parasitic
weeds, the Sannois-La Pagerie homestead looks
the very abode of peace and forgetfulness. A
few steps only from the sea, although it is out
of sight and even out of hearing ; separated
from the town of Trois-Ilets by the Morne
Gantheaume, which cuts off the view, one can

only see around one an amphitheatre of verdure, roofed by a sky whose exquisite transparency is the wonder and despair of the painter. From the extent of the buildings—the erections still standing and the ruins which the eye can make out under the grass—it is possible to judge the former importance of the estate, one of the largest in this once flourishing quarter of the island. On arrival we come first on the dwelling-house, originally constructed on a large scale, as is proved by what remains of its out-buildings ; but it has become since the storm of 1766, and in anticipation of future disasters of the same kind, a simple wooden house. In front of this was a large court planted with tamarinds and sand-box trees, of which a few survive.

" Next comes the sugar-mill with its circle of heavy pillars and its huge roof of red tiles of native manufacture. About it were the sheds containing the cane-refuse destined to heat the refinery furnaces ; the flour-hut where the negroes came to prepare their manioc ; the hospital for the care of the slaves ; and the prison, rarely tenanted on the La Pagerie estate.

"Coming down a few paces from the mill, we reach the refinery, a huge building forty metres long by twenty broad, and divided into several sections for the production of cane-sugar. Alongside the refinery runs a second garden, built up on a terrace. On looking at the monumental solidity of the refinery it is possible to understand how it withstood the terrible storm. During the years which followed, the building was adapted to shelter the La Pagerie family. A low gallery was added on the southern side and rooms were fitted up in the upper part until a new dwelling-house should be erected. A little stream, a mere brook without a name, though its waters were always pure, flowed below the refinery after running through a rock-hewn basin where, according to the Creole custom, M. de Tascher's daughters took their daily bath in the shade of the great mango-trees which protected them from the heat of the sun and from indiscreet eyes. Between this tank and the refinery were the negroes' huts, built in stages on the slope of the hill and surrounded by banana, orange, and bread-fruit trees."

In this home, although her father's circumstances did not allow him to keep it up in any great style, and although the hundred and fifty negro slaves which his daughter's more enthusiastic biographers gave to him probably existed only in their imaginations,[1] Josephine doubtless spent an early childhood of great ease and freedom. The chief charge of her was in the hands of a mulatto woman. This was the demoiselle Marion, *mulâtresse libre de Martinique*, who in an Imperial decree of 1807 received an annual pension of twelve hundred francs from the Emperor in recognition of the care which she had bestowed upon " our well-loved spouse, the Empress of the French, Queen of Italy, during her tenderest infancy." Under the control of Marion it is easy to imagine that Yeyette found life not only easy but idle. Aubenas, as the historian chosen by the family, pictures her learning her early lessons at her mother's side. But she knew little enough when she left school, and her knowledge must have been indeed scanty when she went thither at the age of ten. It may be granted, however, that on one point she had an excellent education

[1] M. Masson, " Joséphine de Beauharnais," p. 35, suggests fifteen or twenty negroes as the more probable figure.

at Trois-Ilets—in the love of nature which was
so marked a characteristic throughout her life.
Amid the lovely surroundings of her home, in
its setting of evergreen wooded hills and West
Indian sky and sea, she did not fail to find an
influence which continued to her death, even
though it might appear to find outward expression principally in the extravagances of the
Malmaison garden.

It was in 1773 that Josephine was sent to
school at the convent of the Dames de la
Providence, Fort-Royal. Her grandmother
Tascher was still living at Fort-Royal, in company with her daughter Marie-Françoise-Rose,
Josephine's "Aunt Rosette." Six years previously Madame Tascher had become a widow.
At the end of 1769 she had surrendered charge
of the little Alexandre de Beauharnais, who was
sent at last to his father in France. When,
therefore, Josephine came to Fort-Royal her
grandmother and aunt were living alone, and
it seems probable that she spent the greater
part of her next four years with them, out of
school hours.

The institution of the Dames de la Providence
was not the best school in Martinique, and

Josephine did not acquire much wisdom there. This was perhaps not altogether the fault of her teachers, for she never showed any of the aptitude for learning which afterwards made her children Hortense and Eugène the pride of the schools to which they were put at Saint-Germain. It was to the accomplishments of music and dancing that Josephine devoted herself with the greatest pleasure at the convent. " A surprising taste for music . . . a very pretty voice," were the points on which her father felt justified in dwelling when writing about his eldest daughter to the Marquis de Beauharnais in January 1778.

Josephine was fourteen years of age [1] when she returned from Fort-Royal and the convent of the Dames de la Providence to her father's home. Into the two following years of her life the more romantic—and unscrupulous—writers who have interested themselves in her career have endeavoured to introduce a love-story or two, feeling no doubt the want of something to

[1] It is usually said in the biographies of Josephine that she remained at school until she was fifteen. But her father's letter of January 9, 1778, to Madame Renaudin, speaks of his eldest daughter " who has left the convent some time." Her fifteenth birthday was not until the following June 23.

give an interest to the very few and bare outlines of the Empress's early life. The efforts
of these romancers hardly deserve notice. There
is only one piece of first-hand evidence, which
is to be found in the memoirs of General Tercier.
Now Tercier, although he claims that " Truth
was always his idol," scarcely inspires much
confidence when he describes his relations with
Josephine. Nor does he say very much. He
is speaking of the year 1778, when he was
twenty-six :

" Young, lively and ardent, I was present at
every fête and gathering of pleasant society.
Among those whom I met was Mademoiselle
Tascher de la Pagerie, the celebrated Empress
Josephine. I was on intimate terms with all her
family. I often spent several days in her mother's
house. She was young then, so was I. . . ." [1]

Subsequent writers appear to have paid particular attention to the dots with which the
passage closes.

A few pages later Tercier records :

" About this time [September 1779] the
vessel *Le Fier*, 50 guns, Commander Turpin,
left for France, carrying on board her who was

[1] Tercier, "Mémoires," pp. 14, 15.

one day to be the Empress of the French. She was eighteen years of age, although the ' Almanach Impérial' always made her out nine or ten years less than she actually was. I accompanied her from Fort-Royal with her family on board the ship. I was, as I have said, very intimate with the family, which escorted her in full force and put her into the captain's hands, with one mulatto woman to wait on her during the voyage."

Now Josephine was not eighteen, but sixteen, when she left Martinique (though she was admittedly well grown for her age), and she did not sail on the *Fier*, but on the *Ile de France*. Moreover, her father and her aunt Rosette accompanied her to France. Tercier's intimacy with the Taschers, therefore, does not seem to have made him a very observant witness of their doings. It is surely unsafe to build too much on the evidence of this idolater of Truth, even when he has recourse to modest dots. The editor of the General's memoirs, M. C. de la Chanoine, states that when Tercier was imprisoned in the Temple as a Royalist conspirator in 1798–9, Josephine used her influence to have him released and so, " by a delicate intervention,

not recorded in the memoirs, repaid the debt
owed by the heart of Mlle. de la Pagerie." One
would not expect Tercier to omit such an incident as Josephine's intervention had it ever
occurred, and M. de la Chanoine's assumption
appears gratuitous.

A wider celebrity has been gained by the
story of the early loves of Josephine and " *l'Anglais*," although the latter, unlike General
Tercier, wrote nothing to perpetuate the legend.
The tradition, however, persisted that there was
a young Englishman in Martinique during
Josephine's girlhood, between whom and her
there was a strong attachment, and that in the
year 1814, when the Allies were in possession
of Paris, this Englishman, who had now risen
to the rank of General, wrote to the ex-Empress
reminding her of their early acquaintance.
Josephine invited him to dinner at Malmaison ;
but on the appointed day she was in her last
illness, and she died without ever having seen
him again. In the pretended memoirs of
Josephine by Mme. Lenormand the name of the
Englishman, or rather Scotsman, is given as
Williams de K——, presumably in order to give
more semblance of reality to the tale !

There is one story of Josephine's Martinique days which stands on a different footing from the boastings of General Tercier or the fairy-tales of Mme. Lenormand. This story appears in many versions, and no doubt she herself told it many times and added to its details as she grew older. But that there was a foundation of truth for it appears from a passage in the memoirs of General Lamarque, whose good faith there seems no reason to doubt. It will suffice to quote Lamarque's words :

" In my childhood I met Josephine at the house of an American lady, Mme. de Hostein, with whom she had been brought up. She was then the wife of Alexandre de Beauharnais, who made himself prominent in the Constituent Assembly by his grace, wit, and patriotic principles. I saw her again several years later when I was commissioned to carry to Paris the flags taken from the Spaniards at the battle of Saint-Martial and at the capture of Fontarabia. She had come out of prison the night before, together with the good Mme. Hostein, and we were dining with the well-known General Santerre, who during his captivity with these ladies had given great care and attention to them. It was now

(*thermidor* 1794) that I heard told for the first
time the prediction made to her by a gipsy
woman that ' she would one day be Queen of
France, but that she would not die a queen.'
' Robespierre nearly upset the prophecy,' she
said with a laugh. Josephine married Bonaparte. He was commander-in-chief of the Army
of Italy, and the world resounded with his
name. Mme. Hostein said to me on her death-
bed, in a feeble voice : ' Well, dear friend, the
gipsy made a mistake about the country. It
is not Queen of France but Queen of Italy that
Josephine will be ! ' " [1]

It does not seem right, therefore, to reject the
story of the gipsy's prediction entirely, common
as such tales are in the histories of those who
rise from insignificance to a throne. But the
elaborate accounts of the meeting between the
Creole girl and the prophetess, with the em-
bellishments of the ladies who took the narrative
from the Empress and put it in their reminis-
cences, need not be accepted too seriously. We
may leave them and turn to the period when
actual documentary evidence begins to be
available.

[1] Lamarque, "Mémoires," i. p. 405.

On October 23, 1777, when Josephine was a
little over fourteen years of age, the Marquis de
Beauharnais in Paris dictated to his seventeen-
year-old son Alexandre a letter in which he
protested his constant attachment and friendship to M. Joseph-Gaspard Tascher de la
Pagerie and proceeded to unfold before him a
scheme which he was satisfied would prove his
sincerity. It was in these words that he set
forth his idea :

" My children now enjoy an income of forty
thousand livres apiece. It lies in your power to
give me your daughter to share the fortune of
my *chevalier*. The respect and affection which
he feels for Madame Renaudin inspire him with
an ardent desire to be united to one of her nieces.
I am only acquiescing in the demand which he
makes of me, I assure you, when I demand your
second daughter, whose age is more suited to his.
I could much have wished that your eldest
daughter had been a few years younger, when
she would certainly have had the preference,
since I have had quite as favourable a picture of
her. But I confess to you that my son, who is
only seventeen and a half, finds a young lady
of fifteen too close in years to himself. This

is one of those occasions on which a sensible
parent is bound to yield to the force of circumstances."

After alluding to Alexandre's qualifications
as a suitor, the Marquis assured his friend that
no dowry would be expected with his daughter,
whom he besought him to bring or send to
France as soon as possible. He wrote also
to Mme. Tascher, apologising to her likewise
for choice of the second before the eldest
daughter.

" It is not [he said] that I have not been told
most agreeable things about the eldest, but my
son finds her too old in comparison with himself. . . . My son is quite worthy of being your
son-in-law. Nature has endowed him with fine
and noble qualities, and his fortune is large
enough for him to share with the woman who
can make him happy. This is what I hope to
find in your daughter, of whom a charming
portrait has been drawn for me. Let her but
resemble you, madame, and I shall have no
doubt about my son's happiness ! "

If the courtly phrasing of the above letters
was the Marquis's and the penmanship Alexandre's, it is not difficult to see that the inspira-

tion was that of a third person. Mme. Renaudin now ruled the life of the Marquis de Beauharnais more firmly than ever. Estranged
from her husband even in Martinique, after her
arrival in France she was not long in returning
to the shelter of the Beauharnais home. But
her friendship with the Marquise, hitherto so
unsuspicious, at last came to an end, and the
household was broken up. As might have been
expected, it was not Mme. Renaudin who de-
parted, but Mme. de Beauharnais. She went
to live with her mother until her death in 1767,
which left the former companion in undisputed
command of the situation and practical controller
of the lives of the Marquis and his younger son.

The fact of Mme. Renaudin's ascendancy over
them explains what would otherwise be difficult
to understand, namely the keen anxiety of both
father and son to obtain the hand of a young
girl whom they had never seen ; a young girl,
too, who had neither money nor exceptionally
good descent to recommend her. Catherine-
Désirée Tascher was not one of the Creole heir-
esses among whom the nobility of France were
wont to look for the means of regilding their
scutcheon, knowing that with the money they

might count also upon winning wives with a
grace and charm which could not be matched
at home among the daughters of rich manu-
facturers. Was not the Marquis careful to
impress upon M. Tascher that he expected no
dowry ?   It was therefore for some other reason
that the alliance was sought, and Mme. Renaudin
alone can supply that reason. This clever
woman had dominated Beauharnais for twenty
years, to the great advantage of herself and her
family, and she had no intention of relaxing her
hold. The union of Alexandre with one of
her nieces would secure part of the Beauharnais
revenues for a Tascher, and to gain her end she
used every means of which she could think.
She impressed upon both father and son the
good points of her nieces, probably persuading
Alexandre to the match during a holiday spent
with her at Noisy-le-Grand, where, with the
fortune which she had accumulated since her
connection with the Marquis, she had taken a
country house for herself at a cost of thirty-
three thousand livres.

Mme. Renaudin probably did not expect any
opposition on the part of her brother ; but she
thought it advisable to point out to him the

desirability of Alexandre. "All that I could tell you about him would be below his deserts," she wrote. "A pleasing face, a charming figure, intelligence, talent, knowledge, and (what is beyond price) all the noble qualities of soul and heart are united in him." Such a character should indeed have grown up into the lofty and patriotic Vicomte de Beauharnais of the Josephine legend. There does not seem much relation between a paragon of the kind described and the actual Vicomte. But then Alexandre was a devoted godson, and his godmother could not but be blind to his faults— especially when making a match for him.

Like her protector, Mme. Renaudin felt that a slight might seem to be inflicted on Josephine by the choice of her sister rather than herself as the bride of Alexandre de Beauharnais, and she wrote to her brother : " It is vexing that your eldest daughter is not at least three years younger than the *chevalier*. But this is not the first time that the younger has been settled before the elder, and we must suppose it to be the will of Heaven, since the age of the second suits better."

It certainly seems strange to the reader of

to-day that the reason for passing over Josephine in favour of Catherine-Désirée should be the age of the former—fourteen years and four months on the day on which the Marquis de Beauharnais and Mme. Renaudin wrote ; and, were there any other real ground for doubting the genuineness of the recognised date of Josephine's birthday, the remarks contained in the letters quoted above might be treated as confirming the doubt. But they appear to have estimated her age roughly as fifteen, or not much more than two years less than Alexandre's. As for Catherine-Désirée, although she was not thirteen at the time when they wrote, still, before she could be married to Alexandre, there must be time allowed for the letters to reach Martinique, for her father to give his consent, and for her to make the journey to France. Perhaps also they contemplated a period of education for the child in Paris, as was proposed later in the case of Marie-Françoise. Moreover, early marriages were not exceptional for Creole girls, usually very advanced for their age, as her father himself described Josephine to be.

It was not for Catherine-Désirée Tascher that

the fate of marrying Alexandre de Beauharnais was reserved. When the proposal for her hand reached Trois-Ilets she had been dead some time. In fact, she succumbed to fever a week before the letters were even written, and her father could only reply that the prospective bride was no more. Not wishing, however, to lose the chance of the honourable alliance offered to him, he suggested to the Marquis that his youngest, Manette (Marie-Françoise), being only eleven and a half, was of an age as suitable to Alexandre as Catherine-Désirée had been. " Her goodness and cheerfulness of character," wrote this accommodating father, " go with a face which will be interesting, and I trust that when a sound education is added she will be worthy of the affection of you and your son."

M. Tascher's letter on the same day [1] to his sister calls for more attention, since it gives us at least a glimpse of Josephine. Would not M. de Beauharnais and his son feel the same sentiments towards his third daughter as toward his second ? he asked.

" It is a sincere attachment to us which gave

[1] Both are dated from St. Lucia, January 9, 1778.

rise to these sentiments, and it may inspire them in one case as in the other. I must tell you that Manette will be well off as regards looks. She unites ingenuous gaiety to a sensible character : education will do the rest. . . . I have spoken to Manette of the journey to France. After many difficulties and regrets about leaving her mother she has at last consented, knowing that she will find a second mother in her dear aunt.

ı "The eldest, who has left the convent some time and who has on several occasions asked me to take her to France, will be a little affected, I fancy, by the preference which I appear to have given to her younger sister. She has a very good skin, good eyes, good arms, and a surprising taste for music. I gave her a teacher for the guitar while she was at the convent, and she made full use of this and has a very pretty voice. It is a pity that she has not the advantage of an education in France. If only I were concerned, I would have brought you two girls instead of one. But how can one part a mother from two daughters at a moment when death has robbed her of a third ? "

M. Tascher was not destined to be disappointed. As he hoped, it was a child, not one

particular child, that was asked of him.   " Come
with one of your daughters or with two,"
replied Mme. Renaudin when she received his
letter.   " Whatever you do will be pleasing to
us. We must have a child from you."

But, in spite of the double chance given to
the father to get rid of a daughter, he was now
confronted by a difficulty which he had not
foreseen. He had hoped to leave Trois-Ilets
in the spring of 1778, taking Manette with him.
At the last moment Manette withdrew her
" consent," supported, or rather instigated, by
her mother and grandmother, and was pros-
trated by a three months' attack of fever, which
was attributed naturally by the two ladies to
the violence which had been done to her
feelings by the attempt to tear her away from
her home. M. Tascher wrote apologetically in
June, the day after Josephine's fifteenth birthday, reminding his sister of the blind attachment which Creole mothers were known to
feel for their children. With some hesitation
he proceeded to play his third card. Failing
the dead child and Manette, there still remained
Yeyette.

" If I had proper means at the moment I

would leave and bring the elder, who is burning
with desire to see her dear aunt. They have
tried to put her on her guard too ; but as she
is more reasonable and has spent part of her
childhood with our mother and Rosette, she is
beyond reach of what has been said to her,
and I am sure of her great desire to know her
dear aunt and to deserve her kindness and that
of M. de Beauharnais. Two reasons have restrained me, however, I must confess : lack of
present means, and her fifteen years. This age
seems to me too close to that of the *cavalier*.
She is, moreover, very advanced for her years,
and during the past five or six months has
grown to look at least eighteen. Apart from
this, she is well enough, of a very sweet disposition, playing the guitar a little, with a pretty
voice and a talent for music, in which she will
soon perfect herself, as well as for dancing.
But I fancy this will not meet your views, which
are of course to train up for yourself a young
person and to make her worthy of the object
who merits our affection as much for his personal
merit as for the gratitude which we owe to his
dear papa." [1]

[1] Letter dated Fort-Royal, June 24, 1778.

If M. Tascher's letter was carelessly composed
and hardly worthy of being read by her whom
her godson proclaimed to be a rival of Mme.
de Sévigné,[1] the writer might at least have
pleaded in excuse his agitation arising from
Manette's defiance of his authority and from his
own "lack of present means," which prevented
him from taking Yeyette to France in place of
her younger sister. Nor did the efforts to aid
him of his sister and the Marquis enable him
to leave Martinique yet. Crossing the letter
to Mme. Renaudin came one from Beauharnais,
sending him an authorisation to publish the
banns of marriage in Martinique, the place for
the name of the bride being left blank. All
that the Marquis insisted upon was that one or
other of the girls should come to France as soon
as possible. He himself might die, he explained,
and his son's guardians might then compel
Alexandre to marry some one else—an argument
in which the anxiety of Mme. Renaudin may
easily be detected. Six weeks later the Marquis
wrote again, stating that Alexandre would prefer
the elder girl as his wife, so that the difficulty
caused by Manette's attachment to her mother

[1] See p. 48.

was removed. " The day of your arrival with your daughter," concluded the letter,[1] " will be a truly happy day for us."

This is the first mention which there is in the correspondence of Alexandre's desire to marry Josephine. But, as a matter of fact, he had expressed his preference for the elder of the two surviving daughters as soon as he heard of Catherine-Désirée's death. When Tascher's letter announcing Manette's refusal to leave her mother was forwarded by the Marquis to Alexandre, then with his regiment near Brest, he replied in a note which deserves quotation for its quaint wording :

" My dear papa," he wrote, " your packet has just reached me. I have read all the letters in it, and I take up my pen at once to answer you. I can imagine the difficulties made by these ladies about sending their daughter to France. They say : ' If the marriage does not take place, there is a journey in vain, and we shall much regret then having separated her from us.' However, one cannot answer for two people who do not know one another pleasing one another, and surely your intention is not to make me

[1] September 9, 1778.

marry this young lady if she and I should feel a mutual repugnance. I do not doubt, after the description which has been given of her, that she will please me. I hope to be so happy as to inspire in her the feelings which I shall experience. There is every reason to conclude that the marriage will be accomplished as we first arranged it, if M. de la Pagerie will bring us the elder of his two daughters. The affection and desire which this young person shows to make her aunt's acquaintance decides me in her favour, and I am already most flattered at having already in common with her the tender feeling which she has for her."

The "young person's" fate was at length decided. As far as the consent of the two fathers and the bridegroom was concerned, all was now clear for Josephine's marriage to Alexandre de Beauharnais. M. Tascher had the banns published in April 1779. Whatever opposition his wife and mother may have made was unavailing. But there was, nevertheless, a very serious obstacle in the way. War between France and England had broken out again, and to cross the Atlantic involved considerable risk of capture. Hence, in spite of the urgent

appeals of Mme. Renaudin, who feared that
the Beauharnais family might interfere or that
Alexandre might grow cold through delay, it
was not until the autumn of 1779 that Josephine
set sail with her father and her aunt Rosette.

The vessel which conveyed the voyagers was
the *Ile de France*, which formed part of a convoy
under the protection of the warship *Pomone*.
The passage of the Atlantic was very rough and
troublesome, but the English at least were
avoided, and on October 20 M. Tascher was able
to write to his expectant sister that he had
reached Brest, very ill, but bringing his elder
daughter with him.

Josephine was thus a little over sixteen years
of age when she landed in France, and the
negotiations had lasted almost two years which
ended in bringing her from Martinique as a
substitute for her two sisters. Some further
delay was still necessary, partly on account of
her father's weakness after the voyage and
partly in order to allow for the publication of
the banns in Paris and the drawing up of the
marriage settlements. In the meantime the
meeting took place between the future husband
and wife—their first meeting, unless they had

seen each other before Alexandre left Fort-
Royal for France at the end of 1769, when he
was nine and Josephine six ; and of this the
correspondence gives no hint. On receipt of
Tascher's letter announcing his arrival, Alexandre had started off with Mme. Renaudin for
Brest, where the encounter took place.

It is unfortunate that no record survives, as
far as we know, of Josephine's first impressions
of France or of her bridegroom ; it is generally
the case throughout her history that we have the
letters to or about her, but not her own letters.
Alexandre's impressions of her are preserved
in a communication to his father, dated Oct. 28.
It is not the letter of an enthusiastic lover,
nor does it convey much idea of her personality
at this period. " Mlle. de la Pagerie," he wrote,
" will perhaps appear to you less pretty than you
expected, but I think I can assure you that the
uprightness and sweetness of her character
surpass all that you can have been told about
it." Six days later he added a postscript to
a letter from Mme. Renaudin to the Marquis :
" The pleasure of being with Mlle. de la Pagerie,
with her to whom the name of ' your daughter '
sounds so sweet, is the only reason for my

silence. It would be hard for me to express
to you how great is her impatience to be presented to you ; and we flatter ourselves that you
feel some desire to embrace two children whose
happiness will consist in working for your
happiness." This is rather more affectionate
than the previous letter, but is still very correct.
Correctness of language and of attitude was the
constant ideal of Alexandre de Beauharnais.
He wished it also to be his wife's ; for he left
it on record some years later that on the very
first day of his meeting with Josephine he
" formed the plan of beginning her education
afresh and of making up by his zeal for the
neglect of the first fifteen years of her life."
A pleasant prospect for the idle young Creole
girl, whose mental development was so far
behind her bodily growth !

The wedding of Alexandre de Beauharnais
and Marie-Joseph-Rose Tascher de la Pagerie
was celebrated on December 13, 1779, at the
parish church of Noisy-le-Grand ; very appro-
priately, seeing that it was here that was the
home of the organiser of the union, the godmother of the bridegroom and aunt of the
bride. The efforts of Mme. Renaudin to bind

together the Taschers and the Beauharnais
had at last been rewarded with a success patent
to all the world. The marriage was a guarantee
that part at least of Alexandre's wealth should
pass securely into the hands of her niece. On
the possessions of Alexandre's father she had
already a firm hold ; and it only remained
for her to give regularity to her position in
the Marquis's house by marrying him herself.
Then the work which she had begun as the
young Creole companion in the Governor's
house at Fort-Royal would be complete. But,
although she became a widow in 1785, she did
not marry the Marquis until 1796, when the
lapse of time might surely have seemed to
render such a step unnecessary.

CHAPTER III

THE VICOMTESSE DE BEAUHARNAIS

AFTER the wedding at Noisy-le-Grand, Alexandre de Beauharnais and his wife went to live in the Paris home of Alexandre's father, situated in the gloomy rue Thévenot—a street which must have been especially depressing to the sixteen-year-old Creole girl, fresh from the sunshine and warmth of Martinique. Of course to the family biographer the situation appears in bright hues. The household, declares Aubenas,[1] was happy from the start.

"With a husband of talent and spirit, brilliant and fêted ; a father-in-law full of affection from the first moment and soon an adorer of the sweetness of her character ; a brother and sister-in-law who asked nothing better than to become her friends ; an aunt whom she loved all the better now that she knew her, and a father gradually recovering the

---

[1] " Histoire de l'Impératrice Joséphine," pp. 102-3.

health of which he had despaired, the young Vicomtesse de Beauharnais might promise herself a charming existence. . . . The first year passed away amid the enchantment of a world both new and curious to her, in the admiration of the marvels of Paris, the hope or the regret of every Creole woman's imagination."

This is the ideal view of affairs ; in reality, the prospect was by no means so brilliant for Josephine. Financially the match was not bad, since, if the income of forty thousand livres which the Marquis had attributed to his son in his first letter to M. Tascher was uncertain, being partly derived from property in distant and unsettled San Domingo, at least it was considerably better than the income upon which the Taschers had lived at Trois-Ilets. Then the Marquis de Beauharnais was certainly an affectionate father-in-law, apart from his willingness to look on the world through the eyes of Mme. Renaudin, who never failed in her devotion to her own family. But, after all, it depended upon her husband whether Josephine was to be happy in her married life ; and Alexandre, young as he was, was not slow to show himself a particularly unpleasing

combination of Don Juan and a pedant.
Gallantry came to him by nature, pedantry by
his education under his tutor Patricol, an
excellently disposed man entirely led astray
by the theories of Rousseau and Raynal. Engaged by the Marquis de Beauharnais to teach
his sons, Patricol had left when the elder of
these entered the army and gone into the
employ of the Duc de la Rochefoucauld as
tutor of his two nephews, the young Rohan-
Chabots. Alexandre was fourteen years of
age when this happened ; and, on the invitation of the democratic Duke, he had followed
Patricol to Roche-Guyon, to be steeped still
further in the atmosphere of Rousseau. Under
Patricol's direction, he continued the worship
of Mme. Renaudin in which he had been trained
in his father's house. At this early age we
find him writing to his godmother beseeching
her to persevere in her letters to him, thereby
at once conferring upon him a great pleasure
and forming his style. "Mme. de Sévigné,"
he assured her, "will no longer be necessary to
me."

At fifteen Alexandre entered the army,
assuming about the same time the title of Vi-

comte, to which his right was very shadowy.
Military life did not undo the effects of his
past lessons, and, to tell the truth, he did not
exert himself after active service. In June
1779, indeed, he contemplated the happiness
of dating letters to his godmother "from
Portsmouth or Plymouth"; but he continued
to write them, instead, in France. As in most
departments of life, Alexandre de Beauharnais
was in his soldiering theoretical rather than
practical.

To such a husband the mentally unformed
Josephine only appealed at first as a subject
for education, and after a short time appealed
not at all. Even Aubenas, with his anxiety to
see all in the best possible light, cannot produce
too plausible an apology for the Vicomte. He
writes : [1]

"Alexandre loved his wife less than she
loved him. The circumstances of their marriage contributed to this state of affairs. The
choice of a bride, made at a distance, almost
at haphazard, and only fixing on Josephine
after temporarily settling on her two sisters;
the marriage of the young girl, hardly a month

[1] "Histoire," p. 109.

after the first meeting, chiefly out of affection
for a godmother and deference to a father ;
her unformed beauty, her rather heavy figure,
not yet suggesting its future consummate
elegance, her imperfect education—all this made
the position a peculiar one, and one whose fruits
were sure to be bitter. When actual possession
had cooled the youthful heat which Alexandre
had mistaken for passion, lukewarmness was
certain to follow soon."

Lukewarmness appears to have followed very
soon indeed. In the spring of 1780 the Vicomte
left his wife to rejoin his regiment. In August
we find him writing to her assuring her of the
pleasure he would have in seeing her again
in a month's time and swearing to her afresh
that he was and had been faithful to her, which
seems somewhat strange. Had Josephine any
ground for suspecting infidelity, or had she
for no reason exhibited extreme jealousy ?
It is difficult to discover any details about her
early married life. There is certainly no evidence to justify the pictures of a brilliant
launch into society which it has pleased some
biographers to paint. If we trusted Imbert
de Saint-Amand, author of numerous works

about Josephine from her first days to her
death at Malmaison, we should believe that the
Vicomte de Beauharnais "introduced his wife
to the best salons of Paris, where she met with
a gracious welcome, since she had already
acquired the gift of pleasing which distinguished
her throughout life." But there is nothing
to show that the Vicomte did anything of the
kind. He could certainly have taken his wife
to Court, had he wished; but Aubenas is
obliged to admit that her name was not to be
found on the list of those presented. What
seems probable is that he considered her unfitted for the society in which he mixed until
she should have educated herself under his
direction; and he grew tired of directing
before Josephine had time to learn. She per-
severed with her "accomplishments," taking
up the harp in place of the guitar on coming
to France, and devoting attention to dancing,
in which her husband was proficient. In other
respects, the burden which Alexandre wished
to lay upon her was too heavy, and it is easy
to imagine that the months which she spent
at the house in the rue Thévenot, with her
father-in-law, aunt, and ailing father, or at

Noisy-le-Grand in the summer, under the eye
of Mme. Renaudin, were far from being as
enchanting as has been assumed by some.

The brilliant society in which she was supposed
to mix probably did not include any more
distinguished people than Alexandre's own relatives, the Vicomte François and his wife, and
the Countess Fanny. François de Beauharnais
the younger was in the opposite political camp
to his brother and was not on intimate terms
with him. The Countess, who had married
in extreme youth but was living apart from the
uncle of François and Alexandre, was one of
the Mouchard family which became prominent
later under the Second Empire, owing to the
patronage of the Empress Eugénie. She was
a woman of literary aspirations rather than
talents, and her novels, plays, and philosophic
poems were much admired by those whom it
paid to admire them, though the uncharitable
said that her lovers were responsible for her
prose and verse. Her visits to the rue Thévenot
doubtless introduced an occasional atmosphere
of polite culture, of a kind which can hardly
have appealed to the unlearned Josephine.

It is only from a few letters again, and none

of them from her own pen, that we are able
to get an insight into Josephine's life at this
period. A characteristic communication from
Alexandre to Mme. Renaudin in November
1780 acknowledges two letters from Josephine
which she had forwarded to him. He "readily
recognised the charm of her style in the first
of these letters," he remarked—from which it
appears that Mme. Renaudin supervised her
niece's writings to her husband. Alexandre
continues :

"You ask my advice as to the course to be
taken about my wife's letters. I will repeat
what I have already said. Were I sure that
she alone had handled the pen I should feel
more pleasure in hearing the flattering things
which she tells me, and should persuade myself
more easily that they came from her heart.
As for the phrasing, I do not care much about
its precision. Besides, to judge by her last
letter, she has made considerable progress and
need no longer blush to write to any one, least
of all to her husband. Try therefore to get
her to take counsel of nobody as to what she
shall write."

Still more interesting and illuminating is a

letter from Alexandre to Josephine herself in the following May : [1]

" I found your two letters charming, *ma chère amie*, particularly the first, since you do not therein make any complaints against me, while in the second you charge me with not showing enough anxiety to tell you about my journey. This undeserved reproach (seeing that I wrote to you the day after my arrival) would affect me if I were not persuaded that it was inspired by friendship. . . . I am delighted at the desire which you manifest that I should instruct you. Such a taste, which is always capable of being gratified, is the source of an ever pure enjoyment and has the precious advantage of leaving no regret behind. If you persist in the resolution which you have formed, the acquirements which will be yours will raise you above others and, adding knowledge to modesty, will make you an accomplished woman," etc. etc.

There is something pathetic in the idea here presented of Josephine, not yet eighteen years of age, craving news of a husband whom she

---

[1] According to Aubenas. We should be tempted to refer it to the May of the previous year after reading Patricol's report opposite.

must somehow have loved and getting instead
such compositions as the above. That she still
loved her husband appears from the hints of
jealousy and also from her desire, which so
pleased the pedant in Alexandre, to be instructed
by him ; since desire for instruction such as
Alexandre wished to impart never manifested
itself at any other period of Josephine's life.

As a matter of fact, the Vicomte de Beauharnais was more estranged from his wife than
could be gathered from the two letters quoted.
The proof of this is to be found in a long account
given by Patricol to Mme. Renaudin of a conversation which he had with his former pupil
during a visit by Alexandre to Roche-Guyon.
Mme. Renaudin had enlisted Patricol's help to
repair the breach which she saw widening between her niece and her godson, and the ancient
tutor on June 5, 1781, thus reported Alexandre's
attitude toward his wife :

" When I first saw Mlle. de Lapagerie [Alex-
andre is represented as saying], I thought that
I could live happily with her. At that moment
I formed the plan of beginning her education
again and repairing by my zeal the neglect of
the first fifteen years of her life. Soon after our

marriage I discovered in her a lack of confidence
which astonished me, since I had done everything to inspire her with that confidence ; and
I confess to you that this discovery rather cooled
my zeal for instructing her. It did not, however, extinguish it. I even tried to excuse her,
and I continued with my plan until at last I
perceived in her an indifference and an absence
of desire to instruct herself which convinced
me that I was wasting my time. I then
renounced my plan and left the education of
my wife to whosoever wished. Instead of remaining at home a greater part of my time with
an object who has nothing to say to me, I am
going out much more often than I intended, and
I am resuming in part the life of my old bachelor
days. I beg you to believe that it is not that
it does not cost my heart dear to renounce the
happiness promised me by my idea of a well-
ordered household. Although I have gone into
the world much since I enjoyed my freedom,
I still have not lost the taste for work. I am
quite ready to put the happiness of a home
and domestic peace before the disturbing pleasures of society. But it seemed to me, acting
thus, that if my wife truly felt friendship for

me, she would make efforts to attract me to her
and to acquire the qualities which I love and
which can keep a hold over me. Well, what
has come to pass is the contrary of what I
expected ; and, instead of my seeing my wife
striving after instruction and accomplishments,
she has become jealous and has developed all
the qualities of that baneful passion. This is
how we stand to-day. It is her desire that in
society I should pay attention to her alone.
She wants to know what I say, do, write, etc.,
and never thinks of learning the true methods
of attaining this end and of winning the confidence which I only keep back with regret and
feel that I shall give her on the first sign which
she gives of her anxiety to become better educated and more lovable."

If we assume Patricol's report of Alexandre's
words to be true (and they certainly sound like
what he might have been expected to say), the
May letter to Josephine cannot have been sincere in its expression of that *amitié* which with
him took the place of conjugal love ; for the
speech to Patricol manifests no sudden decision
to try the effect of neglect upon Josephine.

In sending his report to Mme. Renaudin

Patricol expressed his regret that he could not himself act as Josephine's tutor ; and he recommended that she should devote her attention to the study of literature, history, and geography. But Josephine not only was obliged to do without the instruction of her husband's old teacher ; she found little time to carry out his advice as to study, even if she wished to do so. She returned from her summer season at Noisy expecting a child, and on September 3 she gave birth to a son, who received the names of Eugène-Rose and who afterwards became celebrated as Eugène de Beauharnais, Viceroy of Italy. Alexandre came to Paris to be present at the christening, and the family was in hopes that the advent of a son would reconcile him to his young wife. These hopes were disappointed. Alexandre showed no signs of greater kindness, and Mme. Renaudin, who was not blind to the evil effects of his relapse into the life of his old bachelor days, as the Vicomte himself expressed it, advised him to pay a visit to Italy. It was not hard for her to persuade her godson of the educational advantages of such a journey. He was charmed with the idea of enlarging his mind—and of escaping from the jealousy and lack of intellect shown by his wife. Accordingly Josephine was left once more in the rue Thévenot, with only the additional distraction of her new-born infant to vary the monotony of her days. On the birth of a grandson her father at length made up his mind to return to Martinique. In his two years' sojourn in France he had failed to obtain a much-wished-for increase in his pension from the Government. But, on the other hand, he did obtain the Cross of Saint-Louis ; and from his sister Mme. Renaudin, always ready to share her gains with her family, a loan of twenty-six thousand livres.

When the Vicomte de Beauharnais returned from his doubtless improving trip to Italy at the end of July 1782, he found that his wife and child had removed with his father and Mme. Renaudin to a new home in the rue Saint-Charles, a rather less gloomy house than that in the rue Thévenot. At first the advice of Mme. Renaudin seemed to have worked well, for he was described as enchanted to be with his wife again, and he resumed cohabitation with her. But it was soon apparent that his attitude toward her was unchanged. He seized upon a pretext to rejoin his regiment at Verdun. Aubenas can find nothing better to say than that " his absence, although justified by his military duties, none the less awakened in his wife (prevented from following him by the regulations and by the care of her infant) new attacks of jealousy, which she could not prevent and which Alexandre did not try to assuage by frequent visits." So far from attempting to pay frequent visits to Paris, the Vicomte at the end of September, only two months after his return from Italy, volunteered to join an expedition starting across the Atlantic to relieve Martinique from one of the periodical English attacks. Before he left Brest he was informed by a message from Josephine that she was again with child by him, whereupon he was kind enough to write a letter expressing his happiness at the news—a letter of some considerable importance, as it afterwards proved.

Once more, therefore, Josephine was deserted by the husband of whom she had seen so little— ten months in all, it has been computed—during their three years of married life, and if her affection had succeeded in surviving the cruel tests to which it had been put in that time, she can

have seen him depart with no light heart. The
jealousy which he made one of his complaints
against her was not unjustified. Even his
friendly critics were obliged to admit his exces-
sive gallantry toward the other sex (*une grande
coquetterie avec les femmes* is the expression used
by Aubenas); and if this was so in France,
where his family's sympathy with his wife
restrained him, what was to be looked for when
he was safely across the Atlantic ?

It was not long before the fears which Josephine must have felt were realised. On his
arrival in Martinique, Alexandre paid a visit
to Trois-Ilets, where he found his welcome from
the Tascher family less warm than he may have
expected. His mother-in-law, in particular,
took the opportunity to speak to him in a way
which he did not appreciate. Naturally she
had received from her husband, when he returned
from France, a description of the manner in
which her daughter had been neglected during
the first two years of marriage.

The ostensible reasons for which Alexandre de
Beauharnais had gone to the West Indies were
dissatisfaction with his rank as captain only
and desire for active military service. Un-

fortunately for him, the political situation
changed soon after his arrival, and instead of
war there was peace, under the preliminaries
of the Treaty of Versailles. His time therefore
hung heavily on his hands, and having nothing
better to do he commenced an intrigue. The
object was a Martinique lady, some years his
senior, who had an unknown reason for hating
Josephine, and was well enough acquainted
with her early history to be able to poison her
husband's mind against her. That she should
have been able to do so proves nothing against
Josephine. Beauharnais had never loved his
wife, had already been unfaithful, was bored
with her and had quarrelled with her family;
and Josephine's enemy no doubt expressed
a passion for him which blinded him to the
malice of her insinuations. He gladly believed
whatever monstrous stories were told to him.

The result of the base attack on the unfortunate Josephine's character was soon apparent.
On April 10, 1783, she gave birth to a daughter,
Hortense-Eugénie, afterwards Queen of Holland
and mother of the Emperor Napoleon III. The
news reached the Vicomte in Martinique. After
waiting over three weeks, he wrote to his wife

HORTENSE DE BEAUHARNAIS.
After the painting by Prudhon.   Photo by Levy et ses Fils.

as follows, dropping for once the strain of calm
and self-sufficient philosophy which was generally characteristic of his correspondence :

" If I had written to you in the first moment
of my anger, my pen would have burnt the
paper and you would have believed, on hearing
my invectives, that I had chosen a moment
of ill-temper or jealousy to write to you. But
I have now known for three weeks or more
what I am going to tell you. So, in spite of
my soul's despair, in spite of the rage which
suffocates me, I shall contain myself ; I shall
tell you coldly that you are in my eyes the
vilest of beings, that my stay in this country
has made known to me your abominable conduct
here, that I know the full details of your intrigue
with M. de Be——, an officer in the Martinique
regiment, and that with M. d'H., who sailed on
the *César*, that I am aware of the means you
took to satisfy yourself and the people whom
you employed to get your opportunities ; that
Brigitte was only given her freedom to bind
her to silence, and that Louis, now dead, was
also in the secret ; lastly, I know the contents
of your letters and I will bring with me one of the
presents which you gave. It is too late, there-

fore, for pretences, and, as nothing is unknown
to me, there remains only one attitude for you
to adopt, that of frankness. As for repentance,
I do not ask it of you, you are incapable of it.
A creature who could open her arms to her lover
after the preparations had been made for her
departure, when she knew she was destined to
another, has no soul, is lower than the worst of
hussies. Having been bold enough to reckon
on the slumbers of her mother and her grandmother, it is not surprising that you [*sic*] knew
how to deceive your father also at San Domingo.
I do them all justice and blame no one but you.
You alone could abuse a whole family and bring
scandal and ignominy into a strange family
which you were unworthy to enter. After so
many crimes and atrocious acts, what can one
think of the storms and the wrangles that arose
in our household ? What of this last child,
born eight months and a few days after my
return from Italy ? I am forced to accept it,
but, I swear by the Heaven which enlightens
me, it is another's, strange blood flows in its
veins. It shall never know my shame and, I
take my oath again, it shall never discover
either by its education or by its treatment that

it owes its being to an adulterer. But you
recognise that I must avoid such a misfortune
in future. Make your arrangements, therefore.
Never, never will I put myself in the position of
being abused again ; and, since you are such
a woman as to impose on the world if we lived
under the same roof again, be good enough to
betake yourself to a convent as soon as you
receive my letter. This is my last word, and
nothing in this universe can make me go back
upon it. I will come to see you on my arrival
in Paris, once only. I wish to have a talk with
you and to return something to you. But I
repeat to you : no tears, no protestations. I
am forearmed against all your attempts, and all
my care will be devoted to arming myself still
further against your base oaths, as contemptible
as they are false. In spite of all the invectives
that your fury will pour out against me, you
know me, madam, you recognise that I am kind
and feeling, and I know that in your inmost
heart you will do me justice. You will persist
in denial because from your earliest years you
made falsehood a habit, but you will be none
the less convinced, internally, that you have only
got what you deserve. You probably are not

aware of the way in which I managed to unveil all these horrors, and I shall only tell it to my father and your aunt. It will be enough for you to realise that men are very indiscreet, most especially when they have cause for complaint. Besides, you wrote ; besides, you gave up M. de Be——'s letters to his successor ; and then you employed persons of colour, whose indiscretion one can buy with money. So look upon the shame with which you and I, as well as your children, are about to be covered, as a punishment from Heaven which you have deserved ; it ought to gain for me your pity and that of all honourable hearts.

" Good-bye, madam ; I am writing to you in duplicate, and the two letters will be the last which you will receive from your desperate and unhappy husband.

" P.S.—I leave to-day for San Domingo, and I reckon on being in Paris in September or October, if my health does not break down under the fatigue of a journey in conjunction with so terrible a state of affairs. I imagine that after this letter I shall not find you in my house, and I must warn you that you would discover in me a tyrant if you did not follow my bidding precisely."

The man who wrote the above letter, which it has seemed worth while to quote in full, was the same who had before leaving France expressed his happiness at knowing for certain that his wife was a second time with child. Moreover, he could not well have forgotten that he had returned to Paris at the end of July 1782, and that the child was born on April 10 in the following year. What amount of sincerity there was in the charge with regard to the paternity of Hortense is obvious. As for the other accusations in his abominable letter, he could not well tell Josephine that he had derived his information from his present mistress. But probably he felt no compunction in hiding this fact from one who " from her earliest years had made falsehood a habit."

In August Alexandre de Beauharnais left Martinique, but not without hearing from Trois-Ilets. He had not concealed from his father-in-law with what feelings toward Josephine he was going home. Tascher wrote angrily to him, offering to take his daughter back, and bitterly attacking his conduct in Martinique. " So this is the result of your journey," he said, " and of the fine campaign which you were

counting on making against the enemies of the
State.   You got as far as making war on your
wife's good name and the peace of her family."
For once Joseph-Gaspard Tascher appears in
a vigorous attitude, even if it is only on paper.

Beauharnais arrived in France early in October,
having sent Josephine's traducer ahead of him
to Paris.   The letter of accusation had reached
Josephine at Noisy-le-Grand, during her usual
summer visit, and she had remained in her
aunt's house to await events.   Mme. Renaudin
and the old Marquis had both sent messages to
meet the husband on his landing, urging him
to be reconciled.   But Alexandre was in no
mood for reconciliation.   He merely wrote to
Josephine expressing his astonishment that she
had not yet retired to a convent and assuring
her of the inflexibility of his resolution.

"Could we live together after what I have
learnt ? " he asked.   "You would be made as
unhappy as I by the constant thought of your
misdeeds, which you would know to be familiar
to me.   And, though you would be incapable
of remorse, would not the idea that your husband
had obtained the right to despise you be at
least humiliating to your self-respect ? . . . I

see no reason, if you wish to return to America,
against allowing you to adopt this alternative,
and you may choose between the return to your
family and a convent in Paris."

After stating that he would like to see the little
Eugène, if he were sent to Paris, Alexandre added
that nothing which his wife could do would cause
him to alter his opinion. He feared, perhaps,
that the desire to see Eugène might be inter-
preted as a sign of relenting; and he concluded:

"For the last six months I have spent all my
time in hardening myself on this point. Submit
yourself therefore, like me, to a painful course,
to a separation which will hurt your children
most of all, and be assured, madam, that of the
two of us you are not the one most to be pitied."

We know nothing of any replies which
Josephine may have made to her husband's
letters. On receipt of the last she hurried to
Paris, in spite of his commands. To avoid the
possibility of meeting her, the Vicomte had
not gone to his own home, or rather his father's,
in the rue Saint-Charles, but to two hired houses
in succession, where he received with unwavering
sternness all efforts in the direction of compromise from his father, his godmother, and many

well-meaning friends of the family. At the same time he took proceedings to secure a separation. At length in December, seeing that all attempts to improve the situation were in vain, Mme. Renaudin made a decided step on her niece's behalf. It was customary for ladies in Josephine's position to take refuge in a convent while judicial proceedings were pending. At the abbey of Panthemont in the rue de Grenelle-Saint-Germain at the time were several others in a similar plight. Hither the aunt and niece went to lodge while a counter-case against the Vicomte de Beauharnais was being prepared. There was no difficulty in making out a very strong case. Alexandre's neglect of Josephine had been notorious. They had now been married for four years, during which time he had spent ten months with her. Previous to the Martinique visit he had been neglectful, indifferent, and actually unfaithful. His conduct in Martinique had been worse than ever, and his two letters of July 13 and October 20, 1783, were put in as evidence against him. He had no defence, apart from what he might affect to believe of the stories of his wife's girlhood at Trois-Ilets. With regard to Hortense's legiti-

macy, he had already, as has been seen, destroyed
his own argument by his expression of pleasure
at the prospect of a second child before he left
France for the West Indies. Furthermore, his
family was entirely against him, including his
father, his brother François, and his aunt Fanny
de Beauharnais, who had herself retained the
friendship of the Beauharnais clan, although
separated from her elderly husband Comte
Claude.

There was nothing for Alexandre to do but
to yield to the inevitable. He consented to
meet his wife at the lawyer's office in Paris
on March 3, 1785, and there he withdrew his
accusations against her and consented to a
separation on terms very advantageous to her.
Josephine's victory was complete, and the
Vicomte made no effort to save the situation
for himself. The only stipulation at all in
his favour in the arrangement now made was
that Eugène should pass to his father's custody
after reaching the age of five years. In the
meanwhile the father was to pay for his maintenance as he was to pay for that of Hortense
throughout. He was to allow Josephine five
thousand livres a year, while she was to receive

also the interest on her dowry and might live wherever she pleased. Except by obtaining an absolute divorce from her husband, Josephine could not have triumphed more thoroughly over the unworthy Vicomte, who undoubtedly paid heavily for listening to the slanders of his Martinique mistress and to his own desires to get rid of a wife whom he could not " educate " according to his ideas.

The subsequent history of the married life of Alexandre and Josephine de Beauharnais, down to their practical reconciliation, almost on the foot of the scaffold, is very curious. Writers interested in upholding the family credit of the Beauharnais and the Taschers have naturally tried to minimise the completeness of the estrangement. But the evidence is all against their contentions. As far as Josephine is concerned, it is unnecessary to attempt to show that she overlooked the offences committed against her by her husband. She had been terribly wronged, and her own conduct in the bonds of this unhappy union was in no way to blame, unless her inability to assimilate Alexandre's theories of education must be considered a fault.

CHAPTER IV

THE BEGINNING OF INDEPENDENCE

HITHERTO Josephine's life had not been eventful. Brought up in lazy ignorance until the age of ten ; sent for four years to an indifferent convent school, where she learnt little but music and dancing ; then spending two more years at her father's island home, where she may have had a few childish love affairs ; she had been married at sixteen to a pompous young blackguard, who after a slight effort to train her according to his ideas studiously neglected her and grasped at the first opportunity which he thought he saw of putting her out of his way. Of real education she had none, and of social polish hardly any except what she received from intercourse with her father-in-law and her aunt, and from the occasional meetings with her husband's aunt. Up to the period of her separation she had drifted through life or had been driven by others, inert, helpless, and scarcely articulate. No more unlikely candidate for a throne could well be imagined, few more improbable aspirants to a prominent place in the history of an exceptionably interesting period of time. Part of her insignificance is, of course, due to the fact that we can only see her through the medium of a few letters written by those who directed her fate up to the age of twenty-one, that we never hear her own words or receive any of her personal impressions of what went on around her. But it cannot be denied that during her first twenty-one years of life she gave singularly little promise of deserving the attention of biographers.

It was at the abbey of Panthemont, during her temporary retirement to await the result of the proceedings for a legal separation from her husband, that Josephine first learnt how to hold herself in society and to disguise the deficiencies of her education by reliance on her natural abilities ; that she first learnt, in fact, to be herself as she afterwards became known to the world—the Vicomtesse de Beauharnais who captured the heart of Napoleon Bonaparte.

Her stay at the abbey brought her in contact
with a section at least of the society to which
her husband had not cared to introduce her.
In this convent were to be met members of the
upper classes who had, like her, trouble with
their husbands ; orphans of good family who
had no home to which to go ; and unmarried
ladies whose means did not enable them to live
as well in the outside world, or who liked the
religious air of the place combined with the
liberty which other convents did not allow.
Panthemont was a superior kind of " home
for gentlewomen " of not too reduced circumstances, perfectly respectable and almost aristocratic in tone. Here, with her aunt to guide
her in the choice of her acquaintances, Josephine
spent a profitable year and a quarter, gaining
an insight into the manners of society and
making friendships which were destined to
prove very useful to her afterwards.

In the August following her emergence from
Panthemont, Josephine joined the Marquis de
Beauharnais and the recently widowed Mme.
Renaudin at Fontainebleau. Here the Marquis
had taken a country-house, having given up
the Paris residence and the establishment at

Noisy-le-Grand. His pension from the Government had lately been cut down to a quarter of its size, and he had also lost revenues in San Domingo, where Josephine's father had shown little ability in the management of his friend's estates. Both he and Mme. Renaudin were in ill health and welcomed the idea of a peaceful existence at Fontainebleau. Society, however, was not wholly lacking, if that society was drawn chiefly from the bourgeoisie ; the Comtesse Fanny de Beauharnais had a house close at hand, to give a tone to it ; and there were dances, theatricals, and a hunt to supply Josephine with amusement. With the care of her two children in addition, she found life fuller than it had hitherto been for her. The separation had undoubtedly brought with it an improvement in her lot. Moreover, there was no question of open hostility between herself and Alexandre. There was, rather, a softening of the bitterness which had existed, on one side at least, before husband and wife parted. Gradually there came to be a weekly interchange of letters, in which they gave each other news of their children ; for in September 1786 the five-year-old Eugène went to his father, in

accordance with the arrangement of the previous
year.

This quiet country life might have continued
for some considerable time had it not been for
the increase of the financial troubles of the
family. Not only had the Marquis a dwindling
income, but Mme. Renaudin had lost by her
husband's death, while Alexandre had become
involved in money difficulties and was behind-
hand in his payments to his wife. From
Martinique moneys came in very slowly through
the hands of Joseph-Gaspard Tascher. There
exists an interesting letter from Josephine
to her father partly dealing with this question
—one of the very few of the early letters from
Josephine which have survived. Writing on
May 20, 1787, she says :

" I have received, my dear papa, the bill of
exchange for 2,789 livres which you entrusted
to my uncle. Accept my entire thanks. It
makes me hope that you are seriously trying
to send me soon more considerable sums. This
will be all the more pleasant for me, since they
will bring peace to our minds and prevent us
from making ruinous sacrifices to fulfil our
obligations. You know me well enough, my

dear papa, to be quite sure that but for a press-
ing need of money I should speak to you of
nothing but my fondest affection for you."

She goes on to talk of the little Hortense and
of Eugène in a passage which deserves quotation, as the first example of the affectionate
simplicity with which she, who has by some
been denied the name of a loving mother,
always spoke of her children :

" I am occupied at the moment in looking
after my daughter, whom M. de Beauharnais
wished to be inoculated. I thought I ought
not to oppose his request in this delicate situation : up to the present I have nothing to
reproach myself about, since the child is as
well as could be desired. She is my consolation ;
she is charming in face and in character ; she
already speaks often of her grandpapa and
grandmamma La Pagerie. She does not forget
her aunt Manette, and asks me : ' Mamma, shall
I see them soon ? ' Such is her prattle at the
moment. Eugène has been for four months
at a school in Paris. He is wonderfully well ;
he could not be inoculated because of his seven-
year-old teeth, which are coming early, you see."

This letter, which is signed " La Pagerie de

Beauharnais," after the fashion of the time,
shows Josephine in a kindly, artless light, as
indeed she almost invariably appeared in her
correspondence throughout life.

The " more considerable sums " for which
Josephine hoped did not come over from Martinique, and in 1788 she determined to go on
a visit to her parents. Is it necessary to imagine
a dishonourable reason for her departure from
Fontainebleau ? It has been suggested that
she had intrigues there which made it advisable,
for the sake of her reputation, to leave. It is
impossible to disprove the charge, but, on the
other hand, there is nothing more than a mere
guess upon which to base it. M. Masson writes,
in his " Joséphine de Beauharnais " : " In the
absence of any documents one is reduced to
conjecture ; and the necessity for this mysterious and sudden journey, given the ideas
which can be formed about Josephine's psy-
chology, can only be looked for in one of two
causes : love or debts." In fact, she had either
made herself conspicuous in a love affair or
she feared legal proceedings against her for
debt, and in either case she was compelled to
leave Fontainebleau. Such is M. Masson's

verdict. Josephine might, however, be given the benefit of the doubt—a privilege which is seldom hers. It is true that a journey from France to Martinique, with her daughter of five, seems a rash proceeding if all she wanted was money from her father. But Tascher was both ill and financially involved himself, and desperate measures may have seemed necessary to Josephine. He and his wife, too, had often invited their daughter to come to them after the separation from Alexandre and may well have urged her more strongly of late. Josephine was not totally destitute of natural feeling, as might be imagined from the fact that only a discreditable reason has generally been sought for her journey in 1788.

Whatever her motive, Josephine was anxious to quit France at the earliest possible moment. On her arrival at Havre she lodged at a small house kept by two married people in humble circumstances, by name Dubuc, whose address had been given to her by M. de Rougemont, a banker friend. A Government-owned vessel was proposed to her as her means of reaching Martinique ; but such was her impatience that, hearing that this vessel was not sailing for two weeks and that there was another, privately owned, starting at once, she managed to secure a passage on this for herself and Hortense. The only reminiscence which we find of this period is in the Memoirs of Mlle. Cochelet, who was afterwards attached to the household of Queen Hortense and visited Havre with her in September 1814. They found the home of the Dubucs, now a very old couple, whom Hortense likened to Philemon and Baucis. Mme. Dubuc remembered well the visit of Josephine and her child, and how eager the former had been to sail. She recalled, too, a great storm which had overtaken the ship as it left Havre harbour, and how much the captain (a native of Havre, still living in 1814) had been struck by Josephine's courage—a statement which rather surprises us when we recollect that Josephine was a bad traveller and always complained of *migraine*, even on a land journey.

The two years of Josephine's life following her departure from Havre in June 1788 are without a record and must certainly have been very dull for her. The family at Trois-Ilets was badly off. Her father's health continued very poor. Her sister Marie-Françoise, who, had she not been so young ten years ago, might have had the evil fate of marrying the Vicomte de Beauharnais, was also ailing—in consequence, it was said, of an unfortunate love affair, perhaps the same which had resulted in the birth of her illegitimate daughter, afterwards known as Marie-Bénaquette. Both father and daughter died before long, Joseph-Gaspard Tascher in November 1790, and Marie-Françoise a year later. Josephine, however, left Trois-Ilets before either death had taken place, sailing for France again in September 1790.

Her departure from Martinique was almost as sudden as had been her setting out, and the occasion for it is no better known. Friends of the family attributed it to the reception of the news of her husband's rapid advance to the front rank in the Assembly. According to them, Josephine's early love for Alexandre de Beauharnais had never been extinguished, and she was anxious to rejoin him as soon as he was in a position for her to do so. Some even go so far as to make Alexandre summon her to him—a step which our acquaintance with his character hardly renders probable. Nor

was there any reunion between husband and
wife, as such writers as Imbert de Saint-Amand,
for instance, have imagined, after Josephine's
return with her daughter to Paris. Still, it is
likely that the return was partly influenced by
intelligence of Alexandre's success.

Whatever the attraction in France, there
were assuredly sufficient reasons to drive
Josephine from Martinique. Debt and disease
gripped the Taschers at Trois-Ilets, and social
intercourse for them can hardly have existed.
The whole island was in a state of turmoil
through race feuds between the whites and
blacks, and the spirit of revolution had already
penetrated from France to her West Indian
colonies. Fort-Royal was in the hands of
rebels, and the French fleet had been driven
by the captured guns to leave the harbour.
The commander, who was a friend of the
Beauharnais, offered to give Josephine a passage
across the Atlantic. She accepted and arrived
on board the frigate *Sensible* in so great a state
of distress that clothing was actually provided
for her and Hortense on the voyage. Sympathy, however, was readily extended to them,
and we hear of the child being shod with a pair

of shoes manufactured from a sailor's old slippers, while she delighted all by giving them a negro-dance upon the bridge.

Such was Josephine's last farewell to her birthplace. Her father died bankrupt two months later, her sister followed, and only Mme. Tascher de la Pagerie was left to guard what remained of the family estate, in the company of her illegitimate grand-daughter.

In November Josephine set foot in France once more. She proceeded without loss of time to Paris to await news from her husband as to what she should do. The changes during her absence had been great. Alexandre de Beauharnais, seeing little prospect of rapid promotion in a military career, had devoted himself to politics. His choice seemed a wise one. Attaching himself, like his protector, the Duc de la Rochefoucauld, to the Liberal Aristocrats' party, in the opening days of the Revolution he made good progress. His democratic declarations brought him a name, and he was made first a member of the Provincial Assembly of the Orleans district, and then deputy for Blois in the Etats-Généraux. In November 1789 he was prominent enough to

be chosen as one of the three secretaries of the
Constituent Assembly, on the Military Com-
mittee of which he also served. When his
wife reached Paris, the fluently philosophising
Liberal Aristocrat was well on his way to the
Presidency of the Assembly, which he was to
attain after Mirabeau's death in the following
April.

M. Masson has been at some pains to destroy
the legend of the complete reconciliation between Josephine and Alexandre de Beauharnais,
a legend of which there were even two versions.
"According to one, Alexandre was waiting
impatiently for his wife and was ready to do
anything to expiate his faults. According to
the other, he was not informed of her return,
but obliging friends intervened and he consented to see his daughter and his wife; at
the sight of Hortense dressed like a young
American child he came to himself, recognised
his offspring, and all went well." [1] In reality,
M. Masson points out, there was no reunion.
Husband and wife continued to live apart,
and the terms of the act of separation were
strictly observed. They had, however, friends

[1] " Joséphine de Beauharnais," 177-8.

in common and met in society, speaking to one another when they did so and discussing their children's education, a subject naturally very congenial to the Vicomte.

This limited acquaintance, which hardly deserves even Alexandre's favourite term *amitié*, is very different from the picture drawn by Imbert de Saint-Amand, for instance. That amiable courtier writes that " Josephine experienced one of the greatest joys of her life in seeing her husband come back to the tender sentiments of the first days of their marriage, and she settled down with him in Paris, in the mansion which he then occupied in the rue de l'Université, facing the rue de Poitiers." [1] As a matter of fact, while Alexandre lived in the rue des Petits-Augustins, it was only Josephine and Hortense who lived in the rue de l'Université. In the summer after her return to France she was joined by her son Eugène and went with the two children to stop with the old Marquis de Beauharnais and Mme. Renaudin at Fontainebleau, where they still resided.

Here the continued advance of Alexandre brought with it an increase of respect for his

[1] " La Jeunesse de l'Impératrice Joséphine," 27.

family. Only three days after his election as
President of the Assembly the task fell to him
of announcing that the King and the Royal
family had been "carried away by the enemies
of the common weal." For the moment Alexandre himself almost stepped into the King's
place, and it is recorded that when the boy
Eugène walked about Fontainebleau he was
greeted with cries of "Here comes the
Dauphin !" Alexandre's appreciation of his
position may be seen in a passage from a letter
which he sent to his father on June 27. "
am exhausted with fatigue," he wrote, "but
I find the necessary strength in my courage
and in the hope that, deserving by my zeal a
part of the praises which are showered on me,
I may be able to be of service to the common
weal and to the maintenance of the peace of
the kingdom." The philosopher had no doubts
about his performance of his duty, but looked
upon himself as the patriot duly rewarded by
the attainment of the highest honours.

When the summer came to an end, Josephine
left Fontainebleau ; and her return to Paris
may be regarded as her first real launching
into society. She included among her friends

Fanny de Beauharnais, Mme. de Genlis, Char-
lotte Robespierre, the Prince of Salm-Kyrbourg
and his sister, Princess Amalie of Hohenzollern-
Sigmaringen. The last-named, in particular,
became very intimate with her, and in her
house Josephine and Alexandre must often
have met. She also renewed many acquaintances which she had made at Panthemont.
But there is no proof of the existence of a
Beauharnais *salon* such as that with which the
family biographers would credit Josephine. In
the first place she can hardly have had any
funds on which to maintain a *salon*, her father's
death having caused a further decrease in the
moneys coming from Martinique. Nor could
she expect aid from her husband, impoverished
as he was through the troubles in San Domingo.
Moreover, in September the Constituent Assembly came to an end, and Alexandre, after
three months in a post in the provinces, was
ordered to rejoin his regiment. He obeyed the
order slowly, after writing to the Marquis de
Beauharnais to ask for his fatherly blessing in
the year just about to open, so full of new dangers
for his son. In this letter Alexandre did not
mention either Josephine or the children, which

is perhaps a small piece of evidence against the
theories of those who claim that there had been
a full reconciliation between husband and wife.

The career of the Vicomte de Beauharnais
was approaching its end ; but he was destined
before his fall to add some military honours to
those which he had won in the civil sphere.
For no very successful share in the operations
on the Rhine and in the north of France he
rose successively to be adjutant-general, briga-
dier-general, and chief of the staff at Strasbourg. Perhaps it was to his letters that his
promotion was due, for he continued to pour
out in communications to the new Assembly
his reflections on all that passed around him,
couched in his familiar style, talking ever of
Liberty and of his devotion to his country. In
May 1793 he was made Commander-in-Chief of
the Army of the Rhine, and a month later he
was offered the Ministry of War. This he
declined in a long letter declaring that to a man
of his principles command was nothing, the
honour of defending his country everything.
The Government acquiesced and confirmed him
in his post on the Rhine. But his enemies, who
hated him as a *ci-devant* aristocrat, however

much he might boast of his *sans-culotterie*, were always on the watch, and in July his failure, though at the head of sixty thousand men, to relieve Mayence gave them an opportunity. Alexandre saw his danger and wrote to Paris, resigning his post. Belonging to the proscribed caste, he said, he felt it his duty to remove from the minds of his fellow-citizens all reasons for uneasiness which might arise with regard to him in this time of crisis. He continued to urge the acceptance of his resignation, and finally abandoned his post and returned to Strasbourg, although fighting was in progress at the front. He pleaded illness, his enemies talked of an infatuation for the daughter of a commissariat officer at Strasbourg. In three days' time he returned to the front, where he received a letter from Paris accepting his resignation and ordering him to leave at six hours' notice.

Alexandre retired to his estate at Ferté-Beauharnais, still preaching patriotism and speaking of his prayers for the happiness of his fellow-citizens. The fellow-citizens showed no gratitude, for on March 2, 1793, the Committee of Public Safety ordered his arrest and the seizure of his papers. On April 19, followed the arrest of Josephine, who was described in the warrant as "*la nommée Beauharnais, femme du ci-devant général, rue Dominique 953.*"

Since the autumn of 1791 Josephine had divided her time between the house in the rue Saint-Dominique (otherwise the rue de l'Université), Fontainebleau, and the village of Croissy, whither she was first taken by Mme. Hosten Lamotte, a Creole of Saint-Lucia, who shared with her the expenses of her Paris house. Her stay at Croissy was of importance to her (apart from the fact that now for the first time she saw, and fell in love with, the neighbouring château of Malmaison), since it was here that she met Pierre-François Réal, destined afterwards to become a warm partisan of General Bonaparte in Italy and ultimately the Emperor's chief of police, but at present noted for his rather independent Republicanism. This man introduced Josephine at Croissy to Tallien, whose friendship was soon to prove so useful to her. Perhaps also through his acquaintance with the wife, Réal was induced to oppose the attack on Alexandre de Beauharnais, though he was unsuccessful in saving him from his fate.

The fall of the throne in August 1792, however much it strengthened her husband's position, naturally alarmed Josephine, and she hastened to send away her two children with the Princess Amalie to Saint-Martin in Artois, where the Prince of Salm-Kyrbourg had a country house. Eugène was quickly recalled by his father, who disapproved of Josephine's plan, and was placed at the National College at Strasbourg. During the residence of her children with the Princess, the earliest extant letter from her mother to Hortense was written. As example of Josephine's correspondence with her daughter this document is interesting.

" Your letter," she wrote, " gave me much pleasure, my dear Hortense ; I quite appreciate the sorrow which you show at being separated from your mamma. But, my child, it is not for long ; I hope that the Princess will return in the spring, or I will come and fetch you. Oh ! how clever you will be when you return ; how well the Princess will speak of my little children ! I have no need to bid you love her well. I see by your letter that you are very grateful to her for all her goodness to you and your brother. Prove it to her often, my dear ; this is the way to please me.

" I feel much pain at being separated from you and am not yet consoled for it ; I love my little Hortense with all my heart. Embrace Eugène for me.

" Farewell, my child, my Hortense ; I embrace you with all my heart, and I love you just the same.

" Your fond mother,

" JOSÉPHINE DE BEAUHARNAIS."

Having removed her children to a place of safety, Josephine went to Paris as usual for the winter season, and the list of her acquaintances in society grew larger and larger. The faculty which she was developing for accommodating herself to very varied surroundings proved most useful to her. She managed to be on good terms alike with those in power, with whom her position as wife of Beauharnais no doubt had weight, and with those to whom her own inclinations attracted her, both such of the nobility who still dared live in Paris and those who made the pursuit of frivolous pleasures their chief end, whatever the circumstances of the time. Dangers were threatening on all sides, but Josephine manifested at least no outward alarm

on her own behalf.   Still, it would be interesting
to know what ground M. Masson has for stating [1]
that beside living a double or treble life in
society, she wandered also into less respectable
circles.   " This is the only explanation which
can be given," he says, " of her tranquil confidence in the midst of the perils about her."
It may be an explanation, but where is the
evidence ?   Her subsequent conduct may seem
to render it likely that she was not particular
in the choice of her associates.   But at present
she must have been discreet in her lapses, if
there were lapses, or there would surely be more
than the vague calumnies of her enemies in later
years on which to base a charge against her.

Neither her extensive acquaintances, however, nor her adaptability to circumstances
preserved Josephine from danger long.   The
Law of Suspects of September 1793 required all
good citizens to prove their *civisme*.   It was
necessary also to have a domicile outside Paris
to obtain a certificate.   Josephine decided to
take up her residence at Croissy.   Here she was
joined by Hortense and by Eugène, whose school
at Strasbourg had closed, leaving him homeless.

[1] " Joséphine de Beauharnais," 215.

Further proofs of good citizenship seemed advisable, so Hortense was apprenticed to a dressmaker and Eugène to the carpenter Cochard at Croissy.

Fortified, as she hoped, by her display of *civisme,* and with a duly signed certificate, Josephine returned to the rue Saint-Dominique in January, and began a campaign of solicitation of the influential on behalf of those in whom she was interested. This became one of her greatest hobbies throughout the rest of her life and did perhaps more than anything else to gain for her the title of *la bonne Joséphine.* But her early attempts were hardly fortunate. One letter calls for quotation in full, as an example both of Josephine's " Republican " style and of her outwardly expressed opinion of her husband, though nominally it was a petition on behalf of her sister-in-law, who had been imprisoned in Sainte-Pélagie. François de Beauharnais, the uncompromising monarchist, nicknamed " No-Amendment Beauharnais " owing to his opposition to all proposals and modifications of proposals made in the Assembly to limit the King's power, had joined the *émigrés* in 1792, and his wife was naturally suspect.

Josephine, although never on intimate terms with her sister-in-law, took upon herself to write to Vadier, President of the Committee of Public Safety, in the following strain :

"PARIS, 28 *nivôse*, Year II. of the French Republic, one and indivisible.

"LIBERTY.   EQUALITY.

"Lapagerie-Beauharnais to Vadier, representative of the people,

"Greeting, esteem, confidence, fraternity.

"Since it is impossible to see you, I hope that you will consent to read the memorandum which I attach. Your colleague has told me about your severity, but at the same time he has told me about your pure and virtuous patriotism, and how, in spite of your suspicions concerning the citizenship of the ex-nobles, you always take an interest in the unhappy victims of a mistake.

"I am sure that on reading the memorandum your humanity and sense of justice will lead you to take into consideration the position of a wife in every way unhappy, but only because she belonged to an enemy of the Republic, to Beauharnais the elder, whom you knew and who in the Constituent Assembly was in opposition

to Alexandre, your colleague and my husband.
I should feel much regret, Citizen Representative, if you were to confound in your mind
Alexandre and Beauharnais the elder. I put
myself in your place. You are right in suspecting the patriotism of the ex-nobles, but it is in
the realms of possibility that among them are
to be found ardent friends of Liberty and
Equality. Alexandre has never strayed from
these principles. He has constantly marched
straight ahead. Were he not a Republican, he
would have neither my esteem nor my friendship.
I am an American, and in his family only know
him, and if I were allowed to see you, you would
abandon your suspicions. My household is a
Republican household ; before the Revolution
my children were not different from the *Sans-
culottes*, and I hope that they will prove worthy
of the Republic.

" I write to you frankly, I write as a *Sans-
culotte Montagnarde*. I only lament your severity
because it has debarred me from seeing you and
having a little talk with you. I ask of you
neither favour nor concession, but I claim your
good feeling and humanity on behalf of an
unhappy citizeness. If I have been deceived

in the picture drawn for me of her situation and if she was suspect and appeared to you so, I beg you to pay no attention to what I say to you, for I, like you, am inexorable. But do not confuse your old colleague with another. Be assured that he is worthy of your esteem.

"In spite of your refusal, I applaud your severity as far as I am concerned, but I cannot applaud your suspicions about my husband. You see that your colleague has repeated to me all that you told him : he had doubts, like you, but, seeing that I only lived among Republicans, he ceased to doubt. You would be as just, you would cease to doubt, if you had consented to see me.

"Farewell, estimable citizen, you have my entire confidence.

"LAPAGERIE BEAUHARNAIS.
"46-rue Saint-Dominique, faubourg Saint-Germain."

The effect which this remarkable appeal had upon old Vadier, widely known as "Sixty Years of Virtue," may be gathered from the facts that he was the first to sign the order for the arrest of Alexandre de Beauharnais and that he was the man who insisted so strongly on the existence of the "conspiracies" in prison for complicity in which Alexandre was executed six months later.

From the tone of her letter to Vadier it is clear that Josephine had wind of danger menacing her husband ; and it was but ten weeks after she had written it that Alexandre was taken to Les Carmes. In another six weeks Josephine herself followed him. An anonymous accusation denounced " the *ci-devant* Vicomtesse de Beauharnais, who has many secret means of information in the ministerial offices," and on April 19 an order was made out for the arrest of her and her fellow householder, Mme. Hosten. Two days later two members of the Revolutionary Committee called at 46 rue Saint-Dominique and demanded that Josephine should produce all her papers and correspondence. After an examination of these they certified that they had found nothing inimical to the interests of the Republic, " but on the contrary a number of patriotic letters which can only be to the credit of this citizeness." In a cupboard, however, they discovered a collection of letters of the citizen Beauharnais, which they sealed up for reference. And Josephine and Mme. Hosten were taken to Les Carmes.

CHAPTER V

THE SHADOW OF THE GUILLOTINE

IN the squalid and gloomy prison of Les Carmes, the former convent in the rue Vaugiraud, Josephine spent one hundred and eight days, from April 21 to August 6, 1794 or, according to the revolutionary calendar, the 2 *floréal* to the 19 *thermidor, an II*. In Les Carmes there was collected a herd of seven hundred people, men, women, and even children, of all classes and conditions, from the Prince of Salm-Kyrbourg to followers of the humblest professions. Within the walls all was dirty, damp, and dark. The cells were ill lighted and heavily barred and led into black passages, whereby the wretched prisoners at stated times in the day went to their meals in the ancient refectory, first the men, and then the women ; the former bare-necked and bare-legged, un-shaved and unkempt, the latter clad in a single

JOSEPHINE.

From a photo by W. A. Mansell & Co.   After the painting by Isabey.

p. 100.

robe of cotton stuff. Josephine was lodged in a cell on the first floor, seven and a half by thirty feet in size, with a vaulted roof and an iron-barred window looking out on what was once the convent garden. It was a cell of most dismal associations, for on the wall were the outlines of three swords in blood, made by the Septembrists of 1792 after they had massacred Dulau, Archbishop of Arles, and his fellow-prisoners. The " chamber of the swords," as it was called, was the most grim of all the cells in the whole grim building.

Solitary confinement, however, was not part of the prison system at Les Carmes, rather from lack of space than from considerations of humanity. Josephine shared her room with the Duchesse d'Aiguillon, afterwards Mme. Louis de Girardin. Moreover, there was a certain amount of intercourse between the inmates of the various cells. Josephine and Alexandre de Beauharnais saw one another often enough to effect at last some kind of a reconciliation. From the letters which the two wrote from prison to their children this is clear, and in one Josephine actually tells Hortense of her expectation of meeting her husband in three hours' time.

They appear to have met other captives, too, for their enemies told of Josephine's relations in Les Carmes with General Hoche, arrested eight days before her, and of Alexandre's with a young lady called Delphine de Custine.

Husband and wife were not forbidden to write to their children ; and, on their side, Eugène and Hortense, now aged twelve and eleven respectively, worked their hardest on behalf of their parents. According to the story, they were able to introduce into the prison Josephine's pet pug Fortuné, who was used after this to convey to and fro private messages tucked under his collar. They also addressed petitions in May and June to the Convention and the Committee of Public Safety. Their plea to the Convention on Josephine's behalf is a strange document :

" Two innocent children beg of you, citizen representatives, the freedom of their fond mother, of their mother against whom no reproach can be brought except the misfortune of entering a class to which she has proved that she considers herself a stranger, since she has never mixed except with the best of patriots and the most excellent *Montagnards*. After she had asked for her permit to submit herself to the law of the 26 *germinal*, she was arrested without being able to guess the reason. Citizen representatives, you will not suffer the oppression of innocence, patriotism, and virtue. Restore life, citizen representatives, to two unhappy children. Their age is not meant for sorrow."

Who inspired this appeal, with its protestation of Josephine's contempt for the nobility, for which in reality she exhibited such warm feelings throughout her life? It cannot have been the two children themselves who composed the petition. Probably they wrote it at the dictation of Calmelet, a business man employed by Josephine in many confidential affairs and handsomely rewarded by her in later years.

Such poor efforts could not save Josephine. Neither the citizen representatives nor the Committee of Public Safety were open to appeals to their tender feelings, for they had none. If there was the slightest evidence against an ex-noble, he or she was doomed, and among the Beauharnais papers, if not in Josephine's personal correspondence, there can hardly fail to have been something which might be twisted so as to compromise her. According to a common story, Josephine was one of the people saved by the erratic humanitarian La Bussière, who preserved a number of prisoners' lives, destroying their *dossiers* by the simple method of chewing them up. Josephine herself appears to have believed this story, for she made a point of attending a benefit to La Bussière at the Porte Saint-Martin Theatre in 1803 and of contributing to a fund on his behalf.

The captives in Les Carmes had little hope of escaping death, however. When the question of clearing the over-crowded prison arose, Sixty-Years-of-Virtue, Josephine's " estimable citizen" Vadier, called for drastic measures. His wishes prevailed. Some fifty prisoners were accused of plotting to escape, among them being Alexandre de Beauharnais. All but three were condemned to death, and on July 23 the guillotine ended the life of Josephine's first husband. He left behind him a letter addressed to his wife, but evidently intended also for the publication which it actually received in the journals of the day. As a last monument of the style of Beauharnais that letter is given *I* here :

" All appearances from the kind of cross-examination to which a sufficiently large number of prisoners were to-day subjected show that I am the victim of the villainous calumnies of several aristocrats, so-called patriots from this establishment. The presumption that this infernal plot will follow me as far as the Revolutionary Tribunal leaves me no hope of seeing you again, my friend, or of embracing my dear children. I will not talk of my regrets. My loving affection for them, the brotherly attachment which binds me to you, can leave you in no doubt as to feelings with which, in this respect, I shall take leave of life.

" I equally regret my separation from a country which I love, for which I would have given my life a thousand times, and the fact that not only can I serve her no longer but also she will think me a bad citizen as she sees me torn from her breast. This agonising thought cannot but cause me to recommend to your care my memory. Strive to rehabilitate it by proving that a whole life devoted to the service of one's country and to the triumph of Liberty and Equality must, in the people's eyes, refute the words of hateful calumniators, especially

as they are picked from among the suspects.
This task must be postponed, for during the
storms of a revolution a great nation struggling
to shatter its chains must gird itself about with
a righteous mistrustfulness and fear rather to
overlook the guilty than to strike at the innocent.

" I shall die with a calm which fails not,
however, to be touched by the tenderest affections ; but with a courage characteristic of a free
man, with a pure conscience, and an honourable
spirit, whose most passionate prayers are for
the welfare of the Republic.

" Good-bye, my friend ; find consolation in
my children, console them by instructing them,
and above all by teaching them that it is by
means of virtue and the quality of a citizen
that they must efface the memory of my fate
and recall my services and my titles to the
gratitude of the nation. Good-bye, you know
those whom I love. Be their consoler and by
your care prolong my life in their hearts. Good-
bye ; for the last time in my life I press you
and my dear children to my breast.

" ALEXANDRE B."

It is amusing to read the remarks of Imbert

de Saint-Amand [1] upon the death of the Vicomte de Beauharnais—

"this man who had sacrificed everything for the Republic, this patriot with a true Spartan's language and conduct, Alexandre de Beauharnais, the *grand seigneur*, who on the night of August 4, 1789, had so cheerfully renounced his title of Vicomte and his privileges of birth, this man of the old *régime* who devoted himself with such enthusiasm to the new ideas, this general who commanded so bravely the Republican armies, this aristocrat who made himself a name as a *Sans-culotte* and a *Montagnard*."

The remark " as lying as an obituary " surely seems appropriate here !

The news of Alexandre's execution was not immediately conveyed to his wife. When she heard of it, she broke down completely, whether through grief or in expectation of her own speedy death. One story, preserved by Mlle. Ducrest,[2] maintains that her execution was indeed contemplated and that the gaoler entered her cell and told her that he was about to

---

[1] " La Jeunesse de l'Impératrice Joséphine," p. 48.
[2] " Mémoires," chap. xxxiii.

remove her bed of sacking to give to another prisoner. " What ! " asked her room-mate, the Duchesse d'Aiguillon, " is Mme. de Beauharnais to have a new bed ? " " No ; she will have no need of one," was the answer. But so ill was Josephine that a Polish doctor who was called in only gave her a week more to live. In consequence she was not brought before the Tribunal on the 10 *thermidor* as intended. And on the 9 *thermidor* Robespierre fell. Had he fallen a few days earlier the Vicomte de Beauharnais would have been saved as well as his wife.

Josephine's own account of how the news of the 9 *thermidor* reached Les Carmes is given by Mlle. Ducrest ; and it may be noted that it does not support the story of Josephine's serious illness. This is the account :

" Mme. d'Aiguillon feeling rather ill, I led her to the window, which I opened to give her a little air. I noticed a woman of the people who made a number of signs which we could not understand. She kept on clutching her dress, but we did not know what she meant. Seeing that she still continued, I called out to her : ' *Robe ?* ' She signalled, Yes. Then she

picked up a stone and put it in her skirt, which
she showed to us again, holding the stone in
the other hand. '*Pierre?*' I called to her.
Great was her pleasure at finding that we
understood her. Then putting her *robe* and
the stone together, she made the sign several
times quickly of cutting off her head and began
straight away to dance and clap. This strange
pantomime produced in us a feeling impossible
to express, for we ventured to think that she
was giving us news of the death of Robespierre.
At this moment, when we were thus between
fear and hope, we heard a great noise in the
corridor and the voice of the turnkey calling
to his dog, as he kicked him : 'Get along,
Robespierre !' A few minutes later we saw
coming in our companions in misfortune, who
told us the details of the great event. It was
the 9 *thermidor*."

The removal of Robespierre brought relief
from the fear of immediate death, but it was
not followed at once by the release of the captives in Les Carmes. It was ten days later
before Josephine was set free, and she was
among the earliest to leave the prison. Her
fortune was applauded by her companions, it

was said, and she quitted them amid blessings
from all. Yet, curiously, we are also told
that she was conspicuous at Les Carmes for
the utter abandonment of her grief. She had
already cut her hair short in preparation for
the scaffold, and her loud lamentations caused
the other women to blush for her, deploring,
while pitying, her lack of courage. But, as
M. Masson observes, Josephine's attitude was
more genuine than that of the rest, whose
calm courage was less influential in putting an
end to the Reign of Terror than was her womanly
grief. Had more been like her, the heart of
Paris would have relented sooner.

The credit for obtaining Josephine's release
has been variously attributed. The common
story is that it was due to the Marquise de
Fontenay, afterwards known as Mme. Tallien,
whom many have made Josephine's prison
companion. But Teresia de Fontenay was at
the Petite-Force, not at Les Carmes. She may
have known Josephine; and she left her prison
a week before Josephine left hers, so that it is
not impossible that she might have worked on
her behalf. But there is no apparent reason
why she should have done so. On the other

hand, in the Memoirs of Eugène de Beauharnais it is stated that Tallien himself helped Josephine to freedom. He had met her at Croissy through the introduction of Réal, as we have seen, and after her restoration to liberty was evidently on very friendly terms with her. Moreover, it was much more likely that he, rather than his future wife, should have the power to help her now.

On August 6, 1794, Josephine was a free woman once again, after more than one hundred agonising days with the fear of the guillotine constantly before her. She emerged in poverty and a widow, but with the satisfaction that she had her life and her children left, and that, before his death, the husband whom she had once loved sufficiently to be jealous about him had been reconciled to her. It seems impossible to deny that she must have had feelings of regard remaining for the Vicomte de Beauharnais, for she certainly showed in some ways a respect for his memory which his conduct toward her hardly deserved. She was not by any means an inconsolable widow—that was not in her temperament—but that she took pains in the rehabilitation of his name is beyond

doubt. There is extant a letter written by her
to Debry, member of the Convention, thanking
him on behalf of herself and her children for his
allusion on 12 *fructidor* to the death of Beauharnais.

" The first solace which we have felt in our
misfortune," she said, " has been to hear that
you did justice in the midst of the Convention
to a virtuous Republican who fell a victim to
aristocracy. You have a heart able to appreciate the gratitude of his widow and children.
We honour you for this, and, to enlighten you
still further concerning him whom we mourn,
we send you a copy of his last letter. You
will see that as he approached the end of a
life entirely devoted to the Revolution, and at
a moment when men have no more interest
in hiding their real sentiments, it was a pleasure
to him to expound still further the ardent love
of country which never ceased to animate him."

Still more striking as a testimonial to the
forgivingness of her nature is the step which
Josephine took six years later, when she interested herself in a girl of thirteen years of age
whose only recorded name is Marie-Adelaïde.
This was an illegitimate daughter of Alexandre

de Beauharnais. Her mother is unknown, but it is suggested that she was Josephine's traducer in Martinique, whom Beauharnais had brought back to France in 1783. If this was actually the case, Josephine's return of good for the evil which her husband had done her was remarkable. She put the child under the guardianship of Calmelet, and when she was seventeen gave her, with a trousseau and a handsome dowry, in marriage to a Captain Lecomte. Pardon for the offences of Alexandre de Beauharnais could hardly have gone further.

CHAPTER VI

THE WIDOW BEAUHARNAIS

THE period upon which Josephine entered after her release from Les Carmes is one which adds no credit to her reputation, although it is the period in which she accomplished that which has given her her place in history, the feat of capturing the affections of Napoleon Bonaparte. Her unconscious preparation for the conquest of the heart of a genius was of a kind which would scarcely seem to promise success. The utmost efforts of friendly biographers cannot save her name, even by the complete ignoring of all evidence unfavourable to her manner of life during the years 1794-6. The best that can be said is that this life, while very different from what her eulogists would have us believe it to have been,[1] was not so

---

[1] Aubenas, for instance, claims that during the fifteen months following the 9 *thermidor* Josephine's existence was passed " in a very restrained society composed of the friends

BARRAS.
From a lithograph by Delpeche.

p. 114

bad as personal enemies, anti-Imperialists, and professional scandal-mongers would make it out to be. Happily for her, some of her worst enemies, such as Barras, defeated their own ends by the very blackness of the picture which they painted of her. She was not the most notorious figure in the reign of license which followed the end of the Terror. But she was not, either, one of those who remained inconspicuous by the respectability of their lives.

Josephine's good name had been attacked by a few rumours even before her imprisonment. They were scarcely more precise, however, than the insinuations sure, in an epoch of malicious gossip, to be made against a young woman living apart from her husband. Nor can the association with her aunt have tended to her advantage, whatever the charms of Mme. Renaudin's mind and pen. It seems only just to date Josephine's abandonment of moral propriety from the time when she left Les Carmes, almost resourceless and with two fatherless children on her hands. In her distress she

whom the Revolution had left her and those whom prison had given her." Restraint is a quality of which the traces are hard to discover.

turned to the easiest means at the disposal of a fascinating woman to protect herself against poverty.

Gossip assigned to her General Hoche as her first lover and would make out that she commenced an intrigue with him within the very walls of Les Carmes. It is difficult to see how her relations with him could possibly be close inside the prison. There is a tale of her signalling from her cell to his, by means of a mirror, the number of executions, which, if true, would be an ingenious device rather than a criminal intrigue. Hoche was only four weeks at Les Carmes with Josephine. Arrested eight days before her, he was transferred to the Conciergerie on May 16. He was released two days before her, and on August 16 was appointed Commander-in-Chief of the Army centred at Cherbourg. Although he did not take up his post until the first week in September, it is nevertheless clear that the time in which he and Josephine were supposed to have illicit relations was indeed short. Furthermore, he had only been married in the previous February, and report made him much in love with his young wife. It is doubtful whether very much importance would be at-

tached to the story of Josephine's connection
with him were it not for the assertions of Barras.
Now it cannot be said that a reading of the
Memoirs of this infamous man disposes us to
consider his statements trustworthy evidence.[1]

What Barras says would, indeed, hardly be
worth repeating, except as an example of what
a man of his character could write with an eye
to publication. Speaking of the victim of his
malice at the time when she first met Bonaparte,
he says :[2]

[1] M. George Duruy, editor of the "Mémoires de Barras"
(1895), says in his General Introduction, p. xxix: "It will be
enough to cast one's eyes over the article in the Biographie
[Michaud] and the two letters from Josephine to Barras published by the Commission which undertook the task of hunting
through the papers of the Emperor Napoleon III. after September 4, 1870, to convince oneself that, whatever insinuations the
Memoirs of Barras contain, they reveal nothing that has not
long ago been made public." M. Duruy adds that it is unhappily only too certain that Josephine let herself be carried
away by weakness " until a deep feeling (and one probably
new to her) purified her from these ' vices of the age ' and con-
verted the too readily consoled widow of Alexandre de Beauharnais into the irreproachable consort of the First Consul and
the Emperor. The fact that the coquettish and frivolous
friend of Mme. Tallien could not, without leaving some of her
good name behind, go through an epoch like that of the
Directory, when public morals had sunk so low and feminine
virtue had inevitably been exposed to the influence of the
universal corruption—this fact, whether one likes it or not,
is a part of history."

[2] "Mémoires," II. chap. iv.

" Mme. Bonaparte was reputed to have some influence with me. Some believed that she had been my mistress ; others that she still was. What is certain is that she had been the patient mistress, in the sight of the whole world, of General Hoche *e di tutti quanti*. It is not on that account to be said that she did not love General Hoche more than the others. This can readily be believed. He was our best soldier and one of our handsomest men, more a Hercules than an Apollo in build. Whether or not it was from ambition rather than love—since she deceived him as she deceived the rest—Mme. Beauharnais pushed her pretensions to Hoche so far as to wish him to procure a divorce in order to marry her. . . . He had repulsed with horror this suggestion of a divorce, saying in no uncertain tone to Mme. Beauharnais that a man might temporarily go so far as to take a slut as his mistress, but he would not therefore make her his lawful wife."

Barras continues that, long before Hoche's discussion of the matter with him, the General had discovered that " Mme. Beauharnais did not even respect the sentiment with which she was most penetrated " ; and he pretends to quote a letter in which Hoche writes : " As for Rose " (*i.e.* Josephine), " she must cease from troubling me henceforth.   I relinquish all claims upon her in favour of Vanakre, my ostler "— to whom Barras alleges that Josephine gave a portrait of herself in a gold locket attached to a gold chain.

Finally Barras states that Hoche said to him : " It is owing to my having been in prison with her before the 9 *thermidor* that I knew her so intimately.   This would be unpardonable in a man restored to freedom."

There is no reason to suppose that Barras would scruple to invent conversations with Hoche in support of his aspersions on Josephine, his memoirs betraying numerous traces of similar procedure, especially where Napoleon is concerned.   But the belief in the temporary connection with Hoche does not rest on the assertions of Barras alone.   The story was widely spread.   Not unnaturally, positive evidence is not forthcoming.   No significance surely is to be attached to the fact that Hoche put Eugène Beauharnais upon his staff ; for Hoche had served with the Vicomte on the Rhine and may well have been on friendly terms with the Beauharnais family already, as he evidently was later, when he wrote a letter to the old Marquis in July 1796, in which he spoke of being " unwilling to leave Paris without embracing his dear Eugène." Hoche's reputation, it may be added, was not bad, for the period, although Arnault describes him as having " a face which a man of gallant life might envy."

We may leave for the moment, however, the subject of Josephine's moral conduct (to which it will be necessary to go back when we come to the period of her intimacy with Barras himself), and turn to her general circumstances in the latter part of the year 1794. She found herself in financial straits far worse than she had hitherto experienced. The Vicomte's property had been confiscated and her own resources were temporarily at an end. Even if her mother had had money to send her, not only was the sea in English hands, but Martinique itself had fallen, Fort-Royal being captured in February and the Governor (Rochambeau) capitulating soon afterwards. Josephine's uncle, the Baron de Tascher, had surrendered with his chief and had retired to his estate, while his sister-in-law still struggled against debt at Trois-Ilets.

Josephine does not appear to have been able for some time to acquaint her mother with her painful position, for the first letter discovered by Aubenas is one dated November 20, 1794. In this she announced that she had been a widow for four months, but did not ask for money. According to Aubenas, Josephine was now dependent on charity, and naturally he repudiates the idea that she had recourse to lovers. That she borrowed largely is established. Her principal known creditors were Marie Lanoy, her former *femme de chambre*, and her family ; and a Dunkerque merchant named Emmery, who had probably had dealings in sugar with the Taschers. Emmery was mayor of his town and in a good position, for he agreed to advance quite large sums to Josephine. An excellent testimonial to his kindness to her is to be found in her letter to her mother on New Year's Day 1795, wherein she wrote :

" You have doubtless heard of the misfortunes which have befallen me, leaving me and my children with no means of subsistence except your charity alone. I am a widow, deprived of my husband's fortune, as are his children. You see, my dear mamma, what need I have to come to you. Without the care of my good friend Emmery, I do not know what I should have done. I am too certain of your affection to have the least doubt about the anxiety which you will show to procure me the means of living and of showing my gratitude by paying back what I owe to M. Emmery."

She begged that whatever Mme. Tascher could raise for her, even by disposing of capital, should be sent to Hamburg or London bankers, who could transmit to Dunkerque. Mme. Tascher sent some money, but evidently not very much, for Josephine continued to write for further funds to enable her to meet her obligations. The law of the 8 *pluviôse* afforded her some relief, since it allowed her to recover the property, furniture, clothes, etc., which had been hers and her children's before her imprisonment. She returned, therefore, to a semblance of her former state in the rue de l'Université.

Possibly, if she had now attempted to economise, Josephine might have put her affairs straight. But it is no exaggeration to say that from the moment when she left Les Carmes to the day of her death she was never for a moment free of debt, enormous though the sums were with which she was later furnished. At the present moment it was very easy for her to live beyond her means. Out of the money which Marie Lanoy lent her she hired a carriage, and a good proportion of Emmery's loans was spent on dress, flowers, and the like, although the price of everything, necessaries or luxuries, was extremely high and the value of money very low. Only in the matter of food do we hear of any attempt to cut down expenses. She dined out regularly. Provisions were dear, like everything else in 1795, and guests were expected to supply their own bread. The tale is well known how at the house of Mme. de Moulins, where a place was always laid for her, Josephine alone was allowed to come without bread. She was probably herself responsible for this reminiscence of her poverty, for she was fond in later life of telling how she had once been indebted for her daily bread.

Her departures from Paris were occasioned by her need for money.[1] In July we find her

[1] The whole story of Josephine's financial difficulties in 1795 is an intricate one. Those who are interested in it may be referred to M. Masson's "Joséphine de Beauharnais," chap. xvii., where he goes into the matter very fully. He says

at Fontainebleau, where she persuaded Mme. Renaudin to advance her, in the name of her children, fifty thousand livres in paper-money, unfortunately only worth about one thousand five hundred in cash. Part of this money she was obliged to pay out almost immediately as her contribution to the forced loan of the Year IV. Then in the autumn [1] we see her in Hamburg, on a visit to the banker Matthiessen, who

(p. 256): " It can be gathered how precarious and difficult was Josephine's position during the greater part of the Year III.   It was not until *prairial* [end of April] that she saw a glimmer of light, nor until *messidor* [July] that she obtained help from her aunt ; and how small was that help—the louis d'or of 24 livres was then worth 808 livres in paper-money. It was only at the end of the year, in the second month of the Year IV., that she drew on her mother for 25,000 livres. But of these 25,000 livres how much did she owe to Emmery ? Since 1792 she had lived on her borrowings.   ' You can judge from this,' she wrote to her mother from Hamburg, ' that I am indebted to him for considerable sums.'   And this was not her only debt.   She owed to every one and on all sides.   But this was her element and did not prevent her from living."

It is only fair to add that seven years later she lent Emmery and his partner 200,000 francs and refused to take any interest.

[1] Aubenas makes her visit Hamburg toward the end of October, and gives the date of her letter to her mother as October 30. But according to the short note on p. 143, Josephine was in Paris on October 28 and invited Napoleon to lunch with her on the 29th. Presumably Aubenas would dismiss such notes as apocryphal ; but we have no means of checking his date for the Hamburg letter, which if correct would prove the note attributed to Josephine on p. 143 a forgery.

had married a niece of Mme. de Genlis and was well disposed toward the French. She had asked her mother, as has been mentioned, to remit to Hamburg or London, for greater safety. She now drew on Mme. Tascher, by Emmery's advice, three bills, amounting in all to twenty-five thousand livres.

Between her necessary expenses, such as the contribution to the forced loan, and her outlay on the luxuries always dear to her, Josephine had no difficulty in getting rid of the sums which she managed to raise from various sources.[1] But it cannot be said that she entirely wasted her time, if we take into consideration the social acquaintances which she made. They were decidedly useful, if not from the point of view of character desirable. It was in the latter part of 1794 that she became intimate with the lady known as Mme. Tallien, though it is possible that she may have met her before they both nearly fell victims to the

---

[1] Aubenas's comment seems worth quotation : " So it was to her friends at Dunkerque and Hamburg, to her mother, and not to others, that in her honourable misery the brave mother of a family addressed herself " (" Histoire de l'Impératrice Joséphine," 266). Aubenas does not go into the question how Josephine spent her money.

Terror. The former Teresia Cabarrus was
twelve years Josephine's junior and her superior
in beauty, but had many points of likeness to
her, both being elegant women, fond of luxury
and reckless in expenditure, not too brilliant
in intellect, nor at all scrupulous as to the
way in which they kept themselves afloat in
the very troubled seas of the Revolution.
Teresia was not a native of France any more
than Josephine. Born at Saragossa, she had
divided her childhood between Madrid and
Carabanchel (afterwards the home of the Countess of Montijo and her daughter, the Empress
Eugénie), and had gone to Paris to finish her
education. The old Marquis de Fontenay had
fallen in love with her and married her, but
the Revolution had torn her from him, and
only her fascination of Tallien had saved her
life. She was not contented with being only
Mme. Tallien, and rumour credited her with
many *liaisons* beside that with Barras. One
of her friends was Perregaux, at whose house
the Comte de Gervinus records meeting her in
June 1795, the other guests including Tallien,
Mme. de Beauharnais, and a number of financial
people whom it was doubtless a great advantage

for those whose expenditure exceeded their incomes to know.

The acquaintance with Mme. Tallien was of immense service to Josephine. Mme. Tallien appears to have been remarkably free from jealousy, for she not only allowed Tallien to interest himself in the restitution to Josephine of Alexandre de Beauharnais's property, but also introduced her to Barras, President of the Convention and member both of the Committee of Five and the Committee of Public Safety. At what date the introduction took place is uncertain, but they were intimate in the middle of 1795. Facts are against Aubenas's " brave mother of a family." In August she gave up her home in the rue de l'Université and hired a mansion in the rue Chantereine at an annual rental of 10,000 francs in paper-money. No. 6 rue Chantereine, the property of Julie Carreau, wife of Talma, was not a large house, but it had a stable and a small garden attached to it and required three or four servants to look after it. More furniture was also necessary, and Josephine never furnished on a humble scale. If she had not already been heavily in debt, we might suppose that she used the money

which she borrowed from her aunt in July to
rent and furnish her new house. But this
money was wanted elsewhere. Moreover, at
the same time she decided to send Hortense
to school with the fashionable Mme. Campan
at Saint-Germain-en-Laye and Eugène to the
neighbouring Collége Irlandais. Thus she was
involving herself in large additional expenditure
(and part of it at least cash expenditure) at a
time when her personal resources were particularly scanty. Every one believed her to be
getting the money from Barras ; and there
appears no reason to doubt that this was so.

Barras returned from a mission to the north
just before Josephine took her new house, and
was already master of affairs in Paris, though
he did not actually become a Director until
November 1. In the absence of abler men,
he had sufficient strength to seize for a time
the place which was waiting for some one to
take it. He had just the character to which
the moment offered its opportunity. As A. V.
Arnault writes : " The call for courage and
audacity gave him his chance, which he could
not get before, when he was lost amid a crowd
of people who could talk but could not act."

Barras at least was resolute and not destitute
of personal bravery, as he had proved in his
early career in India and at Toulon. He had,
moreover, a good address and good looks.
That he was unscrupulous did not mark him
off from the other men of his day. His social
preferences did not stand in his way ; in fact,
his tastes were easy to gratify and personally
advantageous to him. Among men he drew
the line against no one, whatever his record or
his reputation, so long as he promised to be
of service. Among women he would associate
only with the well bred and elegant—and,
naturally, the beautiful and yielding. The
Revolution provided him with both needy men
ready to do his bidding and reduced ladies
willing to gratify his desires. He rewarded
both not so much by direct payment as by
helping them to pay themselves through the
introductions which he was able to give them.
Liking so well the accompaniments of power,
the pomp and the luxury, he was not unwilling
that his creatures should share them. This
was the extent to which generosity was developed in a character incapable of true appreciation of the worth of others. Really estimable

traits are not to be looked for in Barras. His
Memoirs show him entirely detestable, a self-
satisfied, slanderous, lying libertine, flourishing
in corruption.

The relations between Barras and Josephine
were perfectly open, though hardly such a
notorious scandal as her enemies make out.
Still it was unfashionable to conceal intrigues
of the kind, especially in private life. Josephine
still had a house at Croissy in the summer of
1795, the rent of which Barras claims that he
paid for her. Her entertainment of her lover
there is recorded by the Chancelier Pasquier
in his "Histoire de mon Temps." Pasquier,
too, had a summer residence at Croissy.

"We had as a neighbour Mme. de Beauharnais," he writes. "Her house was next
ours. She came there but seldom, once a week,
to receive Barras, with the numerous company
which he brought in his train. From morning
onward we used to see baskets of provisions
arriving. Then mounted police began to pass
along the road from Nanterre to Croissy, for
the young Director [1] most often came on horse-
back. Mme. Beauharnais' house, as is usually

---

[1] Pasquier is premature in his bestowal of this title.

the custom among Creoles, had a certain ostentatious luxury, while in the midst of superfluities the greatest necessaries would be wanting. Fowl, game, rare fruits were piled up in the kitchen. It was the period of the utmost scarcity, and at the same time dishes, glasses, and plates were lacking, which they would come to borrow from our humble household."

Barras himself took a country house at Chaillot. That Josephine presided here is proved by the existence of a note of invitation to dinner there in her name, mentioning that citizens Barras and Tallien would be present. This note is dated the 24 *pluviôse an IV*. (February 13, 1796)—less than a month before Josephine's marriage to Napoleon.

The most frequent, if less intimate, meetings, however, between Barras and Josephine were at the Luxembourg after Barras's rise to the post of Director. The Luxembourg, recently changed from a palace to a prison, became again the palatial home of the Directory, though when it was first reoccupied there was not a single piece of furniture in the building, and the Directors were obliged to borrow a table from the hall-porter, on which to write their

message to the Councils. A kind of Court
began rapidly to gather at the Luxembourg,
Barras being, if not the king, at least the leader
of fashion, followed at a considerable distance
by Carnot, who alone of the other Directors
had any social pretensions. Paris had altered
greatly after the end of the Terror, and the
Luxembourg now set the example for Paris.
In the words of Arnault, " gallantry had come
back, and Woman, who had been dispossessed
of her empire under the Convention, began to
resume her sway once more." Woman was
especially prominent at the *salons* of Barras,
where were to be seen among others Mme.
Tallien, Mme. Récamier, the Duchesse d'Aiguillon, and Josephine. The assemblies also
gathered together a most motley crowd of late
Terrorists, ex-aristocrats, *incroyables*, Jacobins,
and even returning *émigrés*, all mixed up together like the guests at a fancy-dress ball.
Every one seemed anxious to forget everything
except pleasure, of which there was certainly
much owing to Paris. No time was lost in
making up the arrears, and the round of unrestrained gaieties was unbroken by any consideration of the general scarcity.

MADAME TALLIEN.

From an engraving after a painting by J. Masquerier.

p. 132.

In such an environment Josephine, now at thirty-two developed into a fascinating woman of the world, very different from the awkward colonial girl of seventeen or eighteen who had wearied Alexandre de Beauharnais, found no difficulty in living a life of luxurious debt, helped by the friendship of the chief of the Directors. Aubenas, it is scarcely surprising to see, rejects all stories of her share in the assemblies and fêtes which charmed and scandalised Paris after the Terror, and says that she is made to take part in them on the strength of apocryphal letters, unsupported by any serious and impartial contemporary witness. Previously to her meeting with Bonaparte he makes her pass a whole year in mourning for her husband. Here Aubenas is, unfortunately, unconvincing. So far from spending her time in mourning for the late Vicomte, Josephine sought consolation only too soon. This must be allowed, even if we credit her with no other lover than Barras, which is contrary to all the gossip of the day. But nothing can explain Barras away, and her misfortune in knowing him, though it doubtless appeared to her at the time a piece of excellent fortune, must leave a permanent stain on her record. In his later venom (caused, it would seem, by the fact that she became Napoleon's wife, for no personal grievance against her can be found), Barras bespatters her without compunction. We have already seen some of his remarks about Josephine. In the same chapter of his Memoirs he compares in his gallant fashion the women with whom he engaged in intrigues and says :

" I must point out a distinction which the acquaintances of Mme. Tallien and Mme. Beauharnais agreed in making between them, namely that the *liaisons* of Mme. Tallien were for her genuine pleasure. . . . As for Mme. Beauharnais, it was the general belief that her relations even with the men whom she most appreciated were not as generous as those of Mme. Tallien. Even though the physical motive appeared to be with Mme. Beauharnais the origin of her relations, her libertinism sprang merely from the mind, while her heart played no part in the pleasure of her body ; in a word, never loving save from motives of interest, the licentious Creole never lost sight of business, although those possessing her might fancy she

was conquered by them and was giving herself
freely."

This would be a terrible indictment, were it
not Barras who makes it.   Unhappily, whatever
poor value one may set on the judgment which
Barras puts into the mouths of " the acquaintances of Mme. Tallien and Mme. Beauharnais,"
one can have but one opinion about a point
which does not suggest itself to Barras, the utter
degradation for Josephine in her association
with such a man.

CHAPTER VII

NAPOLEON BONAPARTE

FROM the autumn of 1795 the history of Josephine becomes more precise, and gossip, so difficult to estimate at its proper worth, gives place more and more to real evidence. The cause of this change is that now at length her path crosses that of Napoleon Bonaparte, in the thirty-third year of her age and the twenty-sixth of his. It was time indeed that the widow Beauharnais should meet some one able to take her fate into his hands and remove her from the life of disreputable luxury to which her levity of character and the pressure of her debts threatened to bind her fast.

At the time when Josephine first saw the man who was to make her an Empress, she had just moved into her new house at 6 rue Chantereine, her ability to pay the rent of which was attributed to the fact that she was mistress, or one

Bonapark

NAPOLEON BONAPARTE.

From the pen drawing by Baron Gros in the Louvre.

of the mistresses, of the leading man in France. She was well known in the foremost society of the day, where she owed her introduction to Barras and the Talliens. She included among her friends Mme. Récamier ; the former Duchesse d'Aiguillon, who had temporarily resumed her maiden name of de Navailles ; Mmes. de Kreny and de Château-Renard, as well as others of less respectable reputation ; [1] and among men, beside the revolutionary leaders, a number of the old nobility, such as Caulaincourt, Montesquieu, Nivernais, and Ségur, formerly French Ambassador to Catherine the Great. She still maintained relations with the older members of her own family, and she kept a brave front toward the world of Paris, not apt to be over-censorious as to a woman's means of livelihood in those days.

The date and circumstances of the first meeting of Josephine and Napoleon are given in a story which has become famous—how at the time of the general disarmament of Paris, consequent on the hostile attitude of forty-three out of the forty-eight sections of the city toward the

[1] "Some of the *demi-monde*," says M. Masson, "whom the astonished little Corsican took for the real *monde*."

Convention's decrees, the Government's agents
called at Josephine's house and attempted to
remove the late Vicomte's sword ; how they
were resisted by Eugène and agreed to let him
appeal to the general in command ; how Eugène
hastened into Bonaparte's presence ; how Bonaparte was touched at the boy's request and
allowed him to keep the sword; and how Josephine called to thank the General next day and
immediately conquered his heart. Barras, who
dismisses the story of the sword as an *historiette
touchante* invented by Napoleon, says that no
arms were taken from the young Beauharnais
or from his mother's house, since she belonged
to " our party " ; and he claims to have remarked to Eugène, who accompanied his mother
to the Luxembourg at the time when the disarmament of the 2 *vendémiaire* was proceeding :
" Your house is not one of those where there is
any idea of taking such a step, Eugène. Besides,
your father's sword is certainly that of a good
Republican." Barras adds the characteristic
comment : " The young man might have been
touched at this remembrance. I was, most
genuinely, Mme. Beauharnais probably least
of all, since Alexandre's widow had not by any

means shown herself inconsolable for the loss of so excellent a citizen." [1]

Napoleon's own version of what occurred may be seen in the " Mémorial de Sainte-Hélène " :

" It was during his command at Paris that Napoleon made the acquaintance of Mme. de Beauharnais. The general disarmament of the sections had been carried out. There appeared at headquarters a young man from ten to twelve years of age, who came to beg the commander-in-chief to return to him the sword of his father, formerly general in the Republican service. This young man was Eugène de Beauharnais,

---

[1] In an autograph note added to M. Duruy's edition of the Memoirs of Barras, but not found in the earlier edition of Barras's literary executor, Saint-Albin, the following account is to be found, which bears some resemblance to the ordinary version of the sword story : " One of my aides-de-camp told me that there was a lady asking for Bonaparte. This lady held by the hand a young man of fourteen to fifteen years of age. I soon recognised Mme. de Beauharnais with her son Eugène. Arms had been taken from her house by error on the day of the troubles, and she had been clever enough to say, through her son, that they belonged to her husband, the late General Beauharnais. . . . She came to me next day as if to refer to me the petition which she had already made—and which had already been granted—for the restoration of the arms. Her real object was to make her way into my society, where she knew that Mme. Tallien had taken first place since the 9 *thermidor*." Barras is not a consistent liar, for this account does not at all tally with the statements in his Memoirs as edited by Saint-Albin.

afterwards Viceroy of Italy. Napoleon, touched
by the nature of this request and by his youthful
grace, granted his request. Eugène began to
weep at the sight of his father's sword. The
General was affected and showed him so much
kindness that Mme. de Beauharnais felt obliged
to call next day to express her gratitude.
Napoleon hastened to return her visit. Every
one knows the extreme grace of the Empress
Josephine and her sweet and attractive manners.
The acquaintance soon became intimate, and
they married without delay." [1]

In spite of the sneers of Barras, there does not
seem sufficient reason for rejecting the date of
the 22 *vendémiaire* (October 14, 1795) as that
of Josephine's introduction to Napoleon. She
had been in possession of the rue Chantereine
house twelve days, and he had made his mark in
Paris nine days earlier. The rising General at
once became one of the most frequent visitors.

---

[1] "Mémorial," ii. 216. The account which Napoleon gave
to Barry O'Meara is practically identical, but concludes :
" I felt so much affected by his conduct that I noticed and
praised him much. A few days afterwards his mother came
to return me a visit of thanks. I was much struck with her
appearance, and still more with her *esprit*. This first impression was daily strengthened, and marriage was not long
in following."

There are no records of the first hours of friendship, but M. Masson in his "Napoleon et les
Femmes," chapter iii., attempts an amusing
reconstruction of the scene which met the young
General's eyes when he entered the rather
meagrely furnished abode of the lady who was
so soon to have him at her feet. Evidences
of former elegance there certainly were, but
many things were woefully lacking. Napoleon,
however, did not come to see the house but its
mistress, and with her he found nothing amiss.
He does not exaggerate when he says that
" the acquaintance soon became intimate." No
further proof is required than the note written
by Josephine and dated the 6 *brumaire* (October
28), fourteen days after the first meeting. In
spite of its brevity, this note can leave no doubt
in the reader's mind as to Josephine's feelings
for Napoleon, or at least as to the opinion which
she wished him to have about those feelings.
She wrote :

    " You come no longer to see a friend who
loves you. You have altogether deserted her.
You do wrong, for she is tenderly attached to
you. Come to-morrow, *septidi*, to lunch with
me. I want to see you and talk with you about

your affairs.   Good-night, my friend, I embrace
you.

" VEUVE BEAUHARNAIS."

The "widow Beauharnais" seems to have
had no reason to reproach her friend again for
staying away from her.   Unfortunately a letter
from him to her is undated, so that we cannot
judge precisely the pace at which their intimacy
proceeded.   The letter seems to belong to the
commencement of the actual *liaison*.

"I awoke full of you," Napoleon wrote.
"Your portrait and the intoxicating evening
yesterday left no rest for my senses.   Sweet and
incomparable Josephine, what strange effect do
you produce on my heart ?   Are you angry,
do I see you sad, are you troubled . . . my
spirit is crushed with grief and there is no rest
for your friend.   But is there any more for me
when I abandon myself to the profound emotion
which overwhelms me and drink in from your lips
and your heart a fire which devours me ?   It
was this night that I discovered how different
are your portrait and you.   You are going at
mid-day.   I shall see you in three hours' time.
In the meantime, *mio dolce amor*, a million

JOSEPH BONAPARTE.
From an engraving after a painting by Vicart.

p. 142.

kisses ; but do not give any to me, for yours
devour my blood."

It looks as if the reference in the words " you
are going at mid-day " may be to Josephine's
visit to Hamburg mentioned in Chapter VI., in
which case Napoleon's letter was written at
some time between Josephine's note of the
6 *brumaire* and her departure to Hamburg.[1]

From the above letters it is clear that love was
very early mentioned between Napoleon and
Josephine.[2] When they first spoke of marriage
is less certain. Bourrienne cannot be considered a very trustworthy witness. His account
of the first occasion on which he heard of
Josephine is that some time after *vendémiaire*
(when he joined Napoleon in Paris) he and
Napoleon were dining at a restaurant, when
the General pointed out to him a young lady
sitting nearly opposite them. What did he

---

[1] See p. 124 and footnote (1). But it is impossible to reconcile Aubenas's date for Josephine's letter to her mother
from Hamburg—October 30—and that of her note to Napoleon,
since we must allow for the time taken to reach Hamburg
from Paris at this epoch.

[2] The first mention of the name of Josephine, by the way,
is in the undated letter from Napoleon. He seems to have
been the first to give it to her. The Bonapartes were fond
of altering names at their caprice.

think of her ? asked Napoleon. Bourrienne's
answer seemed to please him, and he proceeded
to talk much about her and her family and her
amiable qualities. He would probably marry
her, he said, being convinced that the union
would make him happy.

Another letter written by Napoleon, also
unhappily undated, except by the hour " 9
o'clock in the morning," brings the idea of
marriage nearer, though the word is not mentioned :

" I left you carrying with me a painful feeling.
I went to bed in great anger. It seemed to me
that the esteem due to my character ought to
remove from your mind the last thought which
influenced you yesterday night. If it held sway
over your heart, you would be most unjust,
madame, and I most unhappy. So you thought
that I did not love you for yourself ! ! ! For
what, then ? Ah, madame, how greatly I must
have changed ! Could so base a feeling be born
in so pure a heart ? I am still astonished at
it, but less so than at the feeling which, when
I awoke, cast at me your feet, without any
malice against you or any power of will. . . .
But you, *mio dolce amor*, have you slept

well ?   Have you thought even twice of me ?
I give you three kisses : one on your heart,
one on your mouth, and one on your eyes."

The exclamation " So you thought that I
did not love you for yourself " leaves one curious
about the scene of the night before Napoleon's
letter. It is hardly possible that Josephine
can have reproached Napoleon seriously with
loving her for her money, for the supposed
twenty-five thousand livres which she claimed
as her income, but which were assuredly not
substantial enough to meet her already vast
liabilities.   Her perpetual financial embarrassment could scarcely be so well concealed from
him that he could be accused of having imagined
her desirable on account of her wealth.   It is
conceivable that she may have charged him
with wishing to marry her through ambition,
since this was a motive to which he gave some
colour himself.   At the end of the passage just
referred to in Bourrienne's Memoirs, the writer
says : " I gathered from his conversation that
his union with the young widow would probably
aid him in attaining the objects of his ambition.
His ever-growing intimacy with her whom he
loved brought him in contact with the most

influential people of the day and made it easier for him to get his pretensions recognised." Napoleon may have talked thus to Bourrienne in order to disguise the warmth of his passion for Josephine ; but others also at the time of his marriage imputed to him a mingling of ambition with his love.

In connection with the possibility of Josephine's monetary difficulties being kept from Napoleon, another question suggests itself. How could he be ignorant of her relations with Barras ? M. Masson seems to think that he was quite unaware of them and adduces the story told by Barras himself. One day Josephine was being escorted home from the Luxembourg by an aide-de-camp of the Director when she found Napoleon waiting for her. She made a tearful attempt at an explanation, telling him that Barras had previously made love to her, had taken up Mme. Tallien with the idea of rousing her jealousy, had offered to abandon Mme. Tallien for her, and finally had made an attempt on her that very day, whereon she had fainted. Napoleon was for going at once to demand satisfaction from the Director, but Josephine began to excuse him, saying, " His manners are rather rough, but he is very kind and useful ; a friend and nothing more."

This tale resembles many in the Memoirs of Barras : the malice is obvious, but not the truth, and it proves nothing. Napoleon's infatuation for Josephine, however, was so great—as his letters before and after his marriage show—that it is permissible to credit his blindness to the scandal which it was impossible to conceal from ordinary eyes.

Whatever the trouble which inspired the letter of "9 o'clock in the morning," it caused no break in the relations between Josephine and her lover. He was swept along in her train through the society which frequented the Luxembourg and the houses of Mme. Tallien and other stars of the period—a society of reviving courtesy in which the brusque-mannered Corsican must have felt himself strangely out of place. Dearer than his association with her in the circles of the Directory were his visits to the rue Chantereine, when her "extreme grace and sweet and attractive manners" might be displayed for him alone. The end was not long in coming, and to the outside world it may well have seemed sudden. On February 13,

1796, Josephine was inviting guests to a dinner over which she presided in Barras's house in the rue Basse-Saint-Pierre, Chaillot. On February 24 she agreed to marry Napoleon Bonaparte. On the night of March 9 he knocked up the mayor, who had already gone to bed, in his quarters in the second arrondissement of Paris ; and at ten o'clock the marriage was performed. The ceremony was purely civil, and no members of either family were present. Josephine's witnesses were her lawyer Calmelet and Tallien ; Napoleon's, Barras and the youthful Captain Lemarrus, the aide-de-camp who had first brought Eugène Beauharnais to his general. As has already been seen, in order to bring their ages closer together, the bride in signing the register took four years from her thirty-two while the groom added a year and a half to his twenty-five.

There is very little to give a clue to Josephine's true feelings toward the man she was marrying. There is one letter said to have been written by her to some woman friend ; Aubenas rejects it on account of its style, but admits that its sentiments are such as might be expected. It contains the following passage :

" You have seen General Bonaparte at my
house. It is he who desires to be a father
to the orphan children of Alexandre de Beauharnais and a husband to his widow. ' Do
you love him ? ' will be your question. Well—
no ! ' You have an antipathy to him, then ? '
No : but I am in a state of lukewarmness which
displeases me and is considered by the devotee
the worst state of all in matters of religion."

Then there is a record kept by Ségur of a
conversation which he had with her in 1804,
when he told her of the difficulty with which
he first persuaded himself, an old Royalist, to
enter the First Consular household. Josephine
confided in return " her inner struggles and long
repugnances at the end of 1795, in spite of her
inclination for Bonaparte, before she could make
up her mind to marry one whom she herself
called ' General Vendémiaire.' "

In view of Josephine's genuinely Royalist
sympathies (however much disguised in her
sans-culotterie of 1794), there is nothing blame-
worthy in the scruples which she confessed to
Ségur. But the letter quoted above, if genuine,
shows her in a much less favourable light. It
can scarcely surprise us, seeing how she acted

after his departure for Italy. But it certainly shows that she did not " love for himself " the man against whom she had unjustly brought a complaint of similar interestedness. Although the strength of his passion no doubt influenced her, she cannot escape the suspicion of accepting him because he was twenty-five and had already a great future prophesied ; while she was thirty-two, was beginning to fade, had large debts and two children, and her prospects of a good marriage were scanty if she refused the love-blinded Corsican.

For the most part her family and friends approved of the match or offered no opposition to it. Perhaps some of the ex-aristocrats looked doubtfully on " General Vendémiaire." But others knew of the General's expectations. Her aunt, Mme. Renaudin, and the old Marquis de Beauharnais, who were themselves getting married after thirty-eight years' acquaintance, favoured the second marriage of her whom they had seen to suffer so much in her first. The Beauharnais children, perhaps, were less inclined than any to be friendly, especially Hortense. She first met her mother's lover at the dinner at the Luxembourg in January 1796, in commemoration of the King's death. Although not yet fourteen, she was among the guests on the strength of her mother's acquaintance with Barras and his fellow Directors. Among the others present were the Talliens and Bonaparte. Hortense sat between her mother and the General, who talked vivaciously all the time to Josephine, leaning forward across the child and causing her to draw back. " He spoke with ardour and seemed to take sole notice of my mother," says Hortense, recalling the scene. Her first impressions of her step-father were certainly not agreeable, and Mme. Campan records that, when the news reached her later that her mother was to become Mme. Bonaparte, she wept. Both she and Eugène were proud of their father's name and had not been allowed by Josephine to realise how worthless a man he had been. They therefore resented the second marriage, much as Napoleon strove to show that he loved the children of his Josephine. Eugène appears to have conquered his early feelings towards Napoleon first, while in Hortense a degree of fear persisted longer.

One person in Josephine's circle exhibited a suspicion of her future husband which was

pardonable, perhaps even praiseworthy on professional grounds ; namely, her notary Raguideau. Méneval's version of the story, doubtless taken from the mouths of Josephine and
Napoleon, seems preferable to others. A few
days before the wedding Josephine sent for
Raguideau, who arrived in the morning, while
she was still in bed. She had been holding
a *levée*, however, and there were some people
in the room, all of whom retired except one young
man, who went and stood in a window-recess,
where the notary did not see him. Josephine
explained her wishes about the marriage-contract and then asked him what people were
saying. Raguideau told her that the idea of
her marriage with so young a man, with a career
to make, amid the dangers of war, was not
altogether welcomed. He stated that this
was his opinion too, and that, while the General
was no doubt estimable, he had " nothing but
his cloak and his sword." Josephine thanked
him and then called with a laugh to the young
man in the window, who was of course Napoleon.
" General," she asked, " have you heard what
M. Raguideau has just been saying ? "   " Yes,
he has spoken like an honourable man. I hope

that he will continue to look after our affairs, for he has inclined me to put my trust in him." This speech rather disconcerted Raguideau, who had been ignorant of his audience. But he did not suffer for his advice, being rewarded later by the Emperor with a subordinate post in the Government.

Méneval, after telling the story, scouts the addition to it which it has pleased others to make, how that on the day of his coronation Napoleon summoned Raguideau to him and, showing him his mantle and the sword whose hilt was adorned with the celebrated Regent diamond, said : " Raguideau, here is my cloak and here my sword ! " [1]

If there was no serious objection to the Bona- parte-Beauharnais wedding on the side of the bride's friends, it was very different on the side of the bridegroom's. But Napoleon forestalled all opposition by keeping his family entirely in the dark. He did not ask his mother's con- sent nor write to his elder brother Joseph. He

[1] Méneval, "Mémoires," i. 204. If Raguideau actually men- tioned the cape and sword, he was singularly near the truth, for in the marriage-contract the husband " declares that he owns neither lands nor goods beyond his personal wardrobe and his military accoutrements."

hurried Lucien off to join the Army of the North
and even found an excuse for sending Louis out
of Paris. He felt that it would be useless to try
to win over the Bonaparte clan before his
marriage, but, like all lovers, he trusted in being
able to do so afterwards, aided by the beauty
and grace of the lady of his choice. He had
little time at his disposal for their conversion
after March 9, but with that marvellous power
which he always showed of conducting his
private affairs in the midst of the most
arduous public duties, he took the first steps
before he assumed command of the Army of
Italy.

This command in Italy, which took the newly
married General from Paris two days after his
wedding, was, according to some of his enemies,
the bait which made Josephine so attractive to
him. She could influence Barras ; and was
not Barras a large part of the Government ?
Perhaps Josephine herself believed the story,
though it made Napoleon's tribute to her personal fascinations less great ; at any rate, when
it was revived after Napoleon's return from
Italy, she did not take the trouble to deny it.
In the alleged letter of Josephine to a woman

friend, to which reference was made above, the words occur :

" Barras says that if I marry the General he will get him the chief command of the Army of Italy. Yesterday Bonaparte, speaking to me of this favour, which already causes murmurs among his brother officers, although it is not yet granted, said: 'Do they think that I have need of protection in order to make my way? They will all be only too glad for me to give them my protection. My sword is at my side, and with it I shall go far.' "

The doubt as to the authenticity of this letter makes it impossible to draw any conclusion from it. Barras himself was anxious to have the story believed, since it brought him credit for perspicacity with regard to Napoleon's genius, while at the same time it redounded little to the credit of either Napoleon or Josephine. Barras's claim, however, is entirely denied by his colleague Carnot ;[1] and between Carnot and

[1] Carnot says, in his defence of himself against the deputy Bailleul: " It is not true that it was Barras who proposed Bonaparte for the command of the Army of Italy ; it was I . . . and it was only among his most intimate friends that Barras boasted of being the author of the suggestion to the Directory. Had Bonaparte failed, I should have been the

Barras there is no doubt who is the more trustworthy.

Of course Barras was in a position to give early information to Josephine of the promotion which he pretended to have secured for her lover. On February 21, 1796, he congratulated her at the Luxembourg on General Bonaparte's nomination, which was to be made next day. Two days later she and Napoleon were engaged, and in another thirteen they were married, with Barras prominent among the witnesses.

The honeymoon, if it may be called so, lasted two days, during part of which, the legend goes, Napoleon was obliged to shut himself up in a room with his maps, calling out through the locked door that love must be adjourned until after victory. On March 11 he wrote a letter to Letourneur, President of the Directory :

" I have requested citizen Barras to inform

one to be blamed, since I had proposed a young man without experience, an intriguer, and had evidently betrayed my country. The others had nothing to do with war ; it was on me that all the responsibility must fall. Bonaparte was victorious ; so it was Barras who got him nominated ; it was to him that thanks were due ; he was his protector, his defender against my attacks. I was jealous of Bonaparte, I thwarted him in all his plans, persecuted him, blackened his character, refused him all help, and evidently wished to ruin him."

the Executive Directory of my marriage with the citizeness Tascher Beauharnais. The trust in me which the Directory has shown in all matters makes it my duty to inform it of all my actions. This is a new bond to unite me to my country. It is one pledge the more of my firm resolve to look for no safety except in the Republic."

Having written thus, Napoleon bade good-bye to his wife and started for the south. According to Barras, he had the simplicity to commend her to his care. If this be true, no further proof can be wanted of Napoleon's ignorance, astonishing though it may seem, of the relation in which Josephine had stood to the Director.

CHAPTER VIII

FROM THE RUE CHANTEREINE TO ITALY

FROM the point of Napoleon's departure for Italy, Josephine began to receive a series of the most remarkable love-letters ever penned. Mme. de Rémusat says in her Memoirs that these letters "furnished a piquant contrast to the elegant and studied grace of those from M. de Beauharnais." Any one who has read the examples of Alexandre de Beauharnais's epistolatory style quoted in the earlier chapters of this book will agree with Mme. de Rémusat about the piquancy of the contrast, but will probably have a different opinion as to the appropriate description of the Vicomte's letters to his wife.

Napoleon lost no time in beginning his correspondence. After leaving Paris he stopped first at Châtillon on the Seine, the home of the father of Marmont, one of his friends at Brienne. From here he sent Josephine a power of attorney

to handle some moneys coming in to him.   Con-
tinuing his journey, he wrote from Chanceaux
on March 14, telling her what he had done at
Châtillon.   He went on :

" Every moment separates me further from
you, my adorable one, and every moment I find
in myself less strength to bear the separation.
You are the constant object of my thoughts ;
my imagination exhausts itself in guessing what
you are doing.   If I see you sad, my heart is
torn and my grief increases.   If you are gay and
playful with your friends, I reproach you for
forgetting so soon the painful separation of three
days ago.   So you are frivolous, and therefore
you are stirred by no deep feeling !   As you see,
I am not easy to content. . . . Ah, do not be gay,
be a little melancholy, and above all may your
soul be as free from trouble as your body from
sickness !   You know what the good Ossian
says about this.

" Write to me, my loving friend, and write
a really long letter, and receive the thousand
and one kisses of a most tender and true love."

This letter, whose passion makes it at times
incoherent, the young bridgroom addressed by
a most curious error to " The Citizeness Beau-

harnais, 6 rue Chantereine ! " Could anything
more clearly betray his agitation of mind ? But
his actions were calm and sensible enough, and
he found time, amid all the preparations for
taking up his command, to approach the leading
members of his family on behalf of his wife.
He made a stay of two days at Marseilles for
the purpose of seeing his mother, who was still
living there with her daughters, and the fruit of
this visit was a letter from Mme. Letizia Bonaparte to her daughter-in-law. It was March 23
when Napoleon left Marseilles, and his mother
did not write her letter until nine days later,
when she had already, it seems, received a
communication from Josephine. As she was a
bad French scholar and could scarcely write
more than her own name, it is probable that she
had the document drafted for her by Joseph
at Genoa. The letter, so formal in its tone, was
hardly calculated to inspire Josephine with a
great idea of the writer's anxiety to welcome
her into her family. It ran as follows :

" I have received your letter, madame, which
could but increase the estimate which I had
formed of you. My son had informed me of

his happy marriage, and from that moment you had not only my esteem but my approval. To my happiness there is only lacking the satisfaction of seeing you. Be sure that I feel for you all a mother's tenderness and that I cherish you equally with my own children. My son gave me to hope, and your letter confirms this, that you would pass through Marseilles on your way to join him. I rejoice, madame, at the pleasure which your stay here will give me. My daughters join me in anticipating the happy moment of your journey. Meanwhile, be persuaded that my children, following my example, promise you the same friendship and tenderness as they have for their brother. Believe, madame, in the attachment and affection of

"LETIZIA BUONAPARTE MERE."

The letter from Josephine to which this was an answer is, like the great bulk of her letters, missing.

Next to Mme. Letizia, Joseph Bonaparte was the most important among Josephine's new relatives. His first letter followed a few days after his mother's. In the meantime Napoleon, who had reached Nice on March 27, had requested his brother, then engaged in commerce at Genoa, to meet him at Albenga, whence he wrote to Josephine that Joseph was " burning with anxiety to meet her." Joseph's own letter of April 7 was, however, not very ardent in its language.

" Madame," he wrote, " I heard with the keenest interest of your marriage with my brother. The friendship which binds me to him does not allow me to deny the happiness which you will bring him. I am sure of it as he is, from the idea which I have formed of you. Pray believe in the fraternal sentiments of your brother-in-law."

The heads of the Bonaparte clan, therefore, had made the required overtures to the stranger whom its coming leader had introduced into it. It remained to be seen how they would fulfil their promises of affection to her when they had met her face to face. At the present moment the only members of the family who were likely to know anything of the late widow Beauharnais were the three younger sons, Lucien and Louis, who had been in Paris at the time of Napoleon's *liaison*, and Jerome, who after the 13 *vendémiaire* had been sent to

the school where Josephine had placed Eugène.
It is hardly likely that much information from
them had reached Letizia and Joseph Bonaparte.

Josephine was therefore left in Paris, after
two days only of her second essay in married
life, free to spend her time according to her
pleasure.   From her husband she was in receipt
of sufficient money to maintain her position in
the house in the rue Chantereine, if not to cope
with the debts of which Napoleon probably
knew little or nothing as yet—the debts
which her own alleged income of twenty-five
thousand livres, coupled with her borrowings
from Emmery and Marie Lanoy, had been
quite inadequate to meet.   Her two children
were both at school at Saint-Germain-en-Laye,
near Paris.   Eugène was at the Collége Irlandais, which had been started by Patrick Mac-
Dermot, former tutor to Mme. Campan's son ;
Hortense at Mme. Campan's own select academy,
where the principal educated so many future
princesses and ladies of title in the manners
and accomplishments of the old *régime.*

For the moment the new Mme. Bonaparte
had no encumbrances, and she was not slow

to show her appreciation of her life in these circumstances and her reluctance to quit it. She moved in the same circles as before her second marriage, with the added advantage of an assured rank as wife of the commander in Italy. None of her old friends were cast aside. She and Mme. Tallien were inseparable. So they are described by Arnault, who returned to Paris from Marseilles in April 1796, and was introduced by the two ladies to the *salon* of Barras. In his amusing " Souvenirs d'un Sexagénaire " he has much to say about this period. He had been absent from the capital for five months and was much astonished by the changes which he saw. The gaiety of Paris reminded him of the rejoicings after a funeral in some countries. " Every day there was a fête. The public gardens were never empty. Concert-halls and ball-rooms, like the playhouses, were too small for the crowds thirsting for the pleasures of which they had been so long deprived." A curious feature of the times was the " Victim Party," a class of entertainment given by some of the ex-nobles to celebrate the losses in their families during the Terror, at which the guests appeared with

their hair cut short, *coiffés à la victime*, as if
before the guillotine. Still more remarkable
were other extravagances of dress—and un-
dress—described not only by Arnault, but by
all the memoirists of the time. Among the
most prominent figures was Mme. Tallien, who
did not scruple to appear in public in the costume
of Diana, with a short tunic, reaching to her
knees and only partly covering her breasts,
and buskins on her feet. We do not hear of
Josephine in such attire, but she affected the
Greek dress which divided popularity with other
eccentricities of the Directory period, and helped
to lend such an air of carnival to Paris life.

Arnault gives a description of Josephine as
she appeared to him now, which is the more
interesting for being almost the only portrait
of her at the epoch of her second marriage.[1]
She was not the most beautiful woman who
was to be seen at the Luxembourg, he says,
but she was certainly the most amiable.

---

[1] There is another, not so flattering, from the pen of the
Duchesse d'Abrantès, who was far from loving Josephine:
" She was still charming at this epoch [May 1796]. . . . . Her
teeth were frightfully bad ; but when her mouth was shut she
had the appearance, especially at a few paces' distance, of a
young and pretty woman " (" Mémoires," ii. 51).

" Her even temper, the gentleness of her disposition, the kindness which animated her looks and was expressed not merely in her language, but in the very tone of her voice ; her natural Creole indolence, which showed itself in her attitude as well as in her movements, and which she did not entirely lose when exerting herself to render a service—all this gave her a charm which counterbalanced the vivid beauty of her two rivals [Mme. Tallien and Mme. Récamier]. Although she had less brilliance and freshness than the other two, still, thanks to her regular features, her elegant suppleness of figure, and the sweet expression of her countenance, she was beautiful also."

This is an early tribute to the peculiar fascination which Josephine throughout the second part of her life exercised over men willing to admit that there were many whose beauty exceeded hers, and that she was not, to speak strictly, a " beauty " at all. It is unfortunate that we have nowhere any record of Josephine's own opinion of her charms. That she did not underrate them is clear from certain small indications which we find later ; and how could she, when she looked upon the number of her

admirers from her early prime down to the
day of her death ?

For the present, her really great conquest
was one about which she appeared to give herself
very little concern.   Not even her most ardent
eulogists can make her out to have been in
any sense a good wife to Napoleon in 1796.
She may not have been actually unfaithful to
him as yet, although her continued intimacy
with Barras is very suspicious.[1]   But her treatment of his passionate letters and her extreme
unwillingness to join him in Italy show an
indifference to him which would be considered
cynical in any other woman.   He continued
to pour out his love in the most unmeasured
language.   Here are two extracts from letters
written to her during his early days in
Italy :

" You have done more than rob me of my
soul.   You are the one thought of my life.
If I am wearied with the turmoil of affairs, if
I fear the outcome, if men disgust me, if I am
ready to curse life, I put my hand upon my
heart and feel your portrait there ; I gaze
upon it, love fills me with absolute happiness,

[1] Especially in view of the letter quoted on p. 214.

and all smiles on me except the length of time that I see myself separated from my dear one."

"To live for Josephine! That is the story of my life. I work in order to get near you; I kill myself in order to reach you. Fool that I am! I do not see that I am taking myself farther from you."

Napoleon no doubt made a grave error in overwhelming with such protestations the woman whom he had chosen and whose character he knew so little. But this error hardly excuses Josephine for her reception of the protestations. Arnault relates [1] that when she was brought, by the hand of Murat, a command from Napoleon to join him in Italy, she showed it to him together with the other letters which he had sent to her since his departure from Paris, all betraying a most violent passion.

"Josephine was amused at this feeling, which was not devoid of jealousy. I can still hear her reading a passage in which, while seeming to reject the suspicions which obviously tortured him, her husband wrote: 'If it is true, however, beware the dagger of Othello!'

[1] "Souvenirs," ii. 291.

I can hear her say, with her Creole accent, ' *Il est drôle, Bonaparte !* ' "

Josephine never had any reticence about her husband. Whether he amused or vexed her, she must always seek a confidant. Arnault continues :

" The love which she inspired in so extraordinary a man clearly flattered her, although she took matters less seriously than he did. She was proud to see that he loved her almost as much as he loved glory. She enjoyed this glory, daily increasing, but it was in Paris that she liked to enjoy it, in the midst of the applause which resounded about her at each fresh piece of news from the Army of Italy."

An even more curious reminiscence of Josephine's attitude toward her husband at this period is furnished by Bailleul, the deputy.[1] Dining with her one night, he discussed Bonaparte's successes and asked her what she thought of him. " I think Bonaparte a very brave man," she answered. No more. It would be possible to make too much of this careless reply, but at least it cannot be called very sentimental or romantic, as Bailleul says.

[1] " Étude sur les causes de l'élévation de Napoléon," i. 138.

But the victorious general was unaware of the thoughts of his wife in Paris, and his one anxiety was to make her join him in Italy. His messengers to Paris at the end of April were not only heralds of victory to the Directory, but also bearers of requests to his wife. First came Murat, with the text of the treaty concluded with Sardinia ; then Junot, carrying twenty-two standards captured from the Austrians, and with him Joseph Bonaparte, bearing a confidential despatch to the Directors. All of them had messages to the conqueror's wife. Joseph came with a letter of recommendation from his brother. " I have for him the most tender friendship," wrote Napoleon ; " he will, I hope, get the same from you, for he deserves it." Joseph was charged to use his powers of persuasion with the lady whom he was meeting for the first time. It is probable that he and Josephine were at once unfavourably impressed with one another, for it was not long before we see them in opposition, which afterwards developed into lifelong hostility.

By the hand of Junot, the summons to Josephine was, perhaps playfully, peremptory. " You must return with him, do you under-

stand ? " wrote Napoleon. It may be suspected that in her letters Josephine had betrayed her unwillingness to leave Paris. Still
less ready was she to do so now, when the fame
of the victory at Montenotte made her the
recipient of so much reflected glory and personal
admiration. The fêtes in honour of France's
success might well seem to her to centre around
her. Was there any one more conspicuous than
herself at the ceremony of the presentation of
the standards to the Directory on May 9 ? She
was perhaps but one of the three Queens of
Beauty on this occasion, and not the most
beautiful ; but Mmes. Tallien and Récamier
were not the wives of the hero of the hour
like Josephine. When the standards had been
received and the speeches were all over, the
principal actors quitted the Luxembourg in the
midst of a brilliant ovation. Junot, the aide-
de-camp, just made colonel, led out his general's
wife and Mme. Tallien from the Palace into the
sunshine of a most glorious day of May. The
description of the scene may be left to Laurette
Permon, who afterwards became Junot's wife
and Duchesse d'Abrantès :

" It may be imagined that Junot was not a

little proud at giving his arms to these two
charming women. He was then twenty-five.
He was a fine young man and had, in particular,
a most remarkable military carriage. He wore
that day a magnificent hussar uniform (that of
the Berchény hussars), and all that the splendour of such a dress could add to his good looks
had been employed to make the brave young
messenger, still pale from the wounds whose
blood had stained the flags taken from the
enemy, worthy of the army which he represented. As he came out he offered his arm to
Mme. Bonaparte, who, as wife of his commander,
had the right to first place, especially on this
solemn day. He gave the other to Mme. Tallien
and so came down the steps of the Luxembourg
with them. The crowd was immense. People
crushed and jostled to get a better view.

" ' See, it's his wife ! It's his aide-de-camp !
How young he is . . . and how pretty she is ! '

" ' Long live General Bonaparte ! ' cried the
mob.

" ' Long live the citizeness Bonaparte ! She
is good to the poor.'

" ' Yes,' said a stout market-woman, ' she's
really Our Lady of Victories.'

" ' Yes,' said another, ' you're right. But look at the officer's other arm, that's Our Lady of September.' " [1]

Such triumphs as this were dear to the heart of Josephine, and she was loth to forgo them and her easy life in Paris, whatever there might be awaiting her in the Italy to which her husband was calling her. It was difficult to find a pretext, however, for refusing to go—unless she were ill. Very conveniently for her purpose, she fell ill. It is impossible to resist the suspicion that her malady was one of the will, rather than of the body. But to Napoleon it was very real. Letters are extant from him to Joseph and his wife, written when he was at Tortona, in which he shows himself plunged in grief.

" I am in despair," he writes to Joseph, " at learning that my wife is ill. My brain reels, and frightful forebodings agitate my mind. I beseech you to lavish all your cares upon her. . . . If she is well and can make the journey, I

[1] Duchesse d'Abrantès, " Mémoires," ii. 51. The allusion was to the September massacres, and is described by the Duchess as *affreux et injuste*. Mme. Tallien was also nicknamed *Notre-Dame-de-Thermidor*.

ardently long for her to come. I want to see her, to press her to my heart. I love her to madness, and I cannot stay far away from her. If she ceased to love me, I should have nothing more to live for in the world. My dear brother, see that my messenger only stops six hours in Paris and that he returns with new life for me."

And again, to Josephine :

" My life is a perpetual nightmare. A fatal foreboding prevents me from breathing. I cannot see, I have lost more than life, more than happiness, more than peace ; I am almost without hope. I send you a messenger. He will only stop four hours in Paris and will then bring me your answer. Write me ten pages. That alone will console me a little. You are ill, you love me, I have grieved you, you are pregnant, and I cannot see you. I have wronged you so much that I do not know how to atone for it. I accuse you of lingering in Paris, and you are ill there. Forgive me, my dear one, the love with which you have inspired me has robbed me of reason, and I shall never recover it. . . ."

But for our knowledge of the many facts of Napoleon's mind, it would be impossible to believe that the man who was writing these pitiful, self-abasing letters was also conquering Italy, fighting and negotiating as if nothing existed for him except the career of his ambition.

The above letter to Josephine was written on June 15. But before she had time to receive it, Josephine had made up her mind to obey her husband's commands. Her illness was put aside and the suggestion that she was pregnant forgotten for the present. What finally determined her to go to Italy, we do not know. She did not start without letting it be seen that she was still very unwilling. " Her chagrin was extreme," Arnault writes, " when she saw that she had no way of escape. Thinking more of what she was about to leave than of what she was going to find, she would have given up the palace prepared for her reception at Milan, all the palaces in the world indeed, for her house in the rue Chantereine." So he describes her as supping for the last time at Luxembourg with a number of friends—presumably including Barras and the Talliens—and starting away with Fortuné, her dog, and her son Eugène. " Poor woman ! " adds Arnault, " she burst into tears,

she sobbed as though she were going to
torture. She was going to reign like a
queen ! "

The party which set out from Paris for Milan
was no small one. Josephine had with her her
waiting-woman, Louise Compoint, three servants, and Fortuné. As her escort there went
Joseph Bonaparte, Junot, and Murat. The
journey was not altogether as pleasant as it
might have been, if we are to believe the gossip
of the Duchesse d'Abrantès. Josephine, according to this, would have liked Colonel Junot
to pay her attention. He, in his devotion to
his general, would not lend himself to a flirtation
with the general's wife, and to escape vexation
made love to Louise, who was on intimate and
friendly terms with her mistress. The consequence was a falling out between Josephine and
her maid, ending in the latter's dismissal at
Milan. It must be remembered that Mme.
d'Abrantès is always biassed when she writes
about Josephine ; and moreover she was Junot's
wife. If Josephine was impressed by either of
her husband's young messengers from Italy, it
was by the dashing Murat, not by Junot. Murat's attentions to her in Paris had not escaped

notice, and rumour continued to couple his
name with hers after their arrival in Italy until
at last, as we shall see, it reached the ears of
Napoleon himself.

When the party reached Milan, the Commander-in-Chief was away for a few days on
military duty, and the reception of Josephine
was of necessity left to the Duc de Serbelloni,
a great Milanese nobleman and President of the
Directorate of the new Cisalpine Republic, in
whose palace she was to be lodged. Napoleon's
return was marked by great expressions of joy
on his part at the pleasure of seeing her again.
" Once at Milan," writes Marmont (afterwards
Duc de Raguse), " General Bonaparte was very
happy. For at that time he only lived for his
wife ; he had long been in the same condition.
Never had a purer, truer, more exclusive love
possessed the heart of a man, and that a man
of so superior an order."

Quitting her again in a few days in order
to try to preserve Mantua from the advance
of Wurmser and the Austrian army, Napoleon
continued to address to Josephine the most
ardent letters, which Queen Hortense has preserved in her collection. That which most

merits quotation is the one dated Marmirolo, the
29 *messidor* (July 17), in which he says :

"Since I left you I have been constantly
melancholy. My happiness is to be with you.
Unceasingly there go through my memory your
kisses, your tears, your lovable jealousy ; and
the charms of the incomparable Josephine kindle
unceasingly a bright and burning flame in my
heart and my senses. . . . I thought I loved you
a few days ago ; but, since I have seen you, I
feel that I love you a thousand times as much.
Since I have known you I adore you more every
day. This proves that La Bruyère's maxim
that ' Love comes all of a sudden ' is false.
Everything in nature has its course and a different rate of growth. I beg you to let me see
some of your faults. Be less beautiful, less
gracious, less tender, less kind above all ; and
above all never be jealous, never weep ; your
tears drive away my reason and scorch my
blood. . . . Get back your health soon. Come
and join me ; and at least, before we die, let us
be able to say : ' We were happy for so many
days ! ' "

So the letters go on, with their messages about
" kisses as burning as you are cold," " as burning

as my heart, as pure as you," anxious inquiries
about her health, and sad complaints of two days
without a letter from her. As he found himself
unable to return to Milan, he sent for her to
come to meet him toward the end of July at
Brescia, "where the most tender of lovers awaits
you." She came; but hardly had they been
re-united when a fresh move on the part of
Wurmser put them in a dangerous position.
Marching on Mantua, he almost took Napoleon
by surprise. According to what Josephine
herself told Ségur, the Proveditore of Brescia
treacherously attempted to aid the Austrians
by inviting the French commander and his wife
to an evening fête on the day on which they
intended to depart. Josephine said that she
" refused so obstinately that she persuaded
Bonaparte to leave at once." " This happy
inspiration," writes Ségur, " saved them. They
were not four leagues from Brescia when the
Austrians, in concert with the Proveditore, made
a forcible entrance into the town. Had Bonaparte been surprised in the middle of the fête, he
would have been either killed or made prisoner
of war."

Whether it was really due to Josephine's

insistence or not, the escape from Brescia was
decidedly lucky. With a small escort of twenty
men the General reached the neighbourhood·
of Verona, whence he made an attempt to send
his wife into safety by way of the shore of
Lake Garda. But her carriage was fired upon
by an Austrian boat ; and, two of the horses
being killed, she abandoned it and fled in a
local cart to Castiglione, where Napoleon met
her again. The presence of the Austrians at
Brescia cut off direct communication with
Milan, and Josephine's terror was extreme.
She wept profusely, and Napoleon is reported
to have vowed that Wurmser should pay him
dearly for the tears which he had caused. At
last an opportunity was found of reaching
Milan by skirting Mantua, which a French
force was besieging. Josephine passed under
fire again, however, from the walls of Mantua,
and it must have been with extreme relief that
she reached Milan once more. Her husband's
state of mind may be gathered from his letter
of August 10, written as soon as he had reached
Brescia again.

" I am here, my adored one," he says, " and
my first thought is to write to you. Your

state of health and your image have never
ceased to occupy my mind for one moment
during the journey. I shall not be at peace
until I have received letters from you. I
await some impatiently. It is impossible for
you to imagine my anxiety. I left you melancholy, troubled, and half-ill. If the deepest
and tenderest love could make you happy, you
ought to be so. I am overwhelmed with
affairs. Good-bye, my sweet Josephine. Love
me, keep well, and think often, often of me.
" BONAPARTE."

The letters which he hoped for did not come
at once, for four days later we find him complaining of the anxiety caused by their absence.
" You know how dear they are to me. I do
not live when I am far from you ; my life's
happiness is in the society of my sweet Josephine."

It would be possible to quote at great length
from these letters of Napoleon to his wife
during the campaign of 1796, so instructive
are they with regard to his feelings towards
her. But as the letters have long been available
in English to all interested in the story of

Napoleon and Josephine, the temptation must be resisted to do more than refer to those letters which are essential to the understanding of Josephine's history at this time. It is unfortunate that we have none of her replies to the impassioned appeals of Napoleon; for it would be interesting to see how far they deserved his criticism, in his letter dated Modena, October 17, that they were " as cold as fifty and like those of fifteen years of married life." One valuable letter of hers remains, having been discovered by Aubenas among the Tascher family archives; but it was addressed to Mme. Renaudin, now become at length Marquise de Beauharnais. Josephine sent it to Paris by the hand of Serbelloni, in whose palace at Milan she was again lodged. She writes :

" M. Serbelloni will inform you, dear aunt, how I have been received in Italy, fêted wherever I went, by all the princes of Italy, including the Grand Duke of Tuscany, brother of the Emperor. Well, I prefer to be just a nobody in France ! I do not care for the honours of this country. I am very wearied. It is true that my state of health contributes much to my

melancholy ; I am often ill. If happiness could
bring me health, I ought to be well.   I have
the most amiable husband it is possible to
meet.   I have no time to want anything.   My
wishes are all his.   He is all day in adoration
before me, as if I were a divinity ; there could
not be a better husband.   M. Serbelloni will
tell you how much I am loved.   He often
writes to my children, whom he loves very
much.   He is sending to Hortense, by M.
Serbelloni, a beautiful repeater-watch, enamelled
and set with fine pearls ;   and to Eugène a
beautiful gold watch.   Good-bye, my dear aunt,
my dear mamma, be assured of my tenderest
affection.   I will try to send to you a little
money on the first opportunity, for the purpose
for which you have asked it."

Why should Josephine have been so
" wearied " at Milan, where she lived a life of
extreme ease and was in no want of money—
two points of great importance to her at all
periods of her existence ?   Part of the truth
can be gathered from her letter to her aunt.
She was in indifferent health ; and the honours
which were hers in Italy failed to please her
because Italy was not Paris.   She had not

ceased to regret the splendour of Paris, where
amid her own friends she could enjoy the glory
of Napoleon's successes. Moreover, it is impossible to resist the idea that the husband
" all day in adoration before her "—even when
he was not within many miles of her—added
to her weariness. In Paris, when she read his
fervent protestations, she might complacently
say : " *Il est drôle, Bonaparte !* "   But in Italy
it was not sufficient to pass over the matter
so lightly, and to answer the many letters with
an occasional reply. She did not write more
frequently from Milan than from Paris, perhaps,
but there was the inevitable meeting with her
husband to be faced, as it had already been
faced for a few days at Milan and at Brescia.
It is only by ignoring the facts that her admiring biographers can present a picture of
her at this period as a woman in love with her
husband. On the other hand, her love for
some one else was a subject of common talk
in Milan and in the army at the time.

The man whom scandal assigned to her as
a lover was a certain Hippolyte Charles, a
friend of Leclerc, who had recently made him
his assistant adjutant-general.   Among the

crowds of young officers who had been presented
to the wife of the Commander-in-Chief on her
arrival at Milan, Charles had especially caught
her attention by his superficial attractions.
Arnault, who came across him earlier in 1796,
declares that he " never met a better companion
nor one of more equable temperament." The
Duchesse d'Abrantès describes him at greater
length. He was a friend of Junot as well as
of Leclerc, so that she had opportunities for
studying him. In appearance Charles was
small but well built, with a brown complexion,
jet-black hair, passable eyes and teeth, and
very small hands and feet. In his elegant
hussar costume, abundantly covered with gold
lace, he was "charming." In society his wit
was not of the kind which appealed to all.
He was much addicted to puns and similar
forms of humour. "A more comical man
could not be found," says the Duchesse. Such
as he was, Charles appealed not only to the
poet Arnault and the Duchesse d'Abrantès,
but also to Josephine, who was not satisfied
with admiring his social talents. She quickly
made an intimate friend of him, and the fact
did not escape public notice that in Napoleon's

absence he was a most constant visitor at the
Serbelloni palace.

Rumour did not at once acquaint Napoleon
with the gossip of Milan, and if expressions of
jealousy are to be found in his letters of September, October, and November 1796, they
are but vague accusations of neglect and
coldness. Definite suspicion was not aroused
in his mind until after the victory of Arcoli
had enabled him to return to Milan. On the
4 *frimaire* (November 24) he wrote a few
hurried lines from Verona, saying that he
hoped soon to be in the arms of her whom he
" loved to madness," and that only Josephine's
love was wanting to make her husband happy.
Three days later he wrote to Genoa from Milan :

" I reached Milan, I hastened into your room,
I left everything to see you and press you in
my arms. . . . You were not there. You are
off to the towns with their fêtes, you fly from
me when I come, you no longer think of your
dear Napoleon. Caprice caused you to love
him, inconstancy makes you indifferent to
him.

" I shall be here until the 9th," he concludes.
" Do not put yourself out. Rush after plea-

sures. Happiness was made for you. The whole world is too happy if it can give you pleasure, and your husband alone is very, very unhappy."

A still more pitiful letter followed next day, ending with the words : " I reopen my letter to give you a kiss. Oh, Josephine, Josephine ! " The self-abasement of a conqueror could hardly have gone further. Josephine returned from Genoa to be forgiven, which did not take long. Her absence from Milan had been due to accident, not to design. She had received an invitation from the old republic of Genoa to be present at some festivities, and, not expecting that Napoleon would reach Milan so soon, had accepted. She came back when the festivities were over, and found little difficulty in persuading her husband that she was rejoiced to see him. Having spent less than a dozen days with her since their marriage, he was easily cajoled. Harmony was completely re-established, and no clouds seemed to mar the brightness of life at the Serbelloni palace. Lavalette, who had just become one of the General's aides-de-camp, writing of this period, says : " The Commander-in-Chief was then in the full intoxication of his married life. Mme. Bonaparte was charming, and all the troubles of command, all the cares of government of Italy, could not prevent her husband from abandoning himself freely to his domestic happiness."

Lavalette adds a little story of the time which is worth repetition: "It was during this short stay at Milan that the young painter Gros made the first portrait of the General. He represented him on the bridge of Lodi at the moment when, flag in hand, he hurled himself forward to inspire the troops. The artist could not get a moment's audience, but Mme. Bonaparte took her husband on her knees after breakfast and held him there for a few minutes." And in this way the portrait was painted.

The examples are many of the similar exercise by Josephine of her power over her husband, and she undoubtedly rejoiced in its exhibition. It is true that in most instances the power was used in obtaining trivial favours, and that where she attempted to use it in more important matters she failed. But there was one great exception to this rule. It was not for nearly fourteen years that she was unsuccessful in exerting her fascination over Napoleon to the extent of making him believe that she was the wife necessary to his happiness. Neglect [1] of him in his absence, and first suspicion, then actual certainty of her infidelity, could not estrange him any longer than for the time when he was out of the circle of her witchcraft.

The story connecting Josephine's name with that of Charles did not yet apparently reach Napoleon's ears, although the hussar is said to have accompanied her to Genoa on the trip which prevented her from being at Milan on November 27. It required the intervention of a third party to drive him to take action.

---

[1] Imbert de Saint-Amand suggests a rather amusing theory with regard to Josephine's neglect of her husband. " It is not impossible," he writes (" La Citoyenne Bonaparte," 121), " that Josephine's coldness was calculated. There are indeed men who are attached more by resistance than by yielding and who unwittingly prefer a variable sky, now splendid, now black and vexed by lightnings, to love's unclouded blue. Let us not forget that Josephine had to deal with a conqueror, and that love resembles war. She did not surrender, she let herself be conquered. Had she been more tender, more attentive, more loving, perhaps Bonaparte would have loved her less."

CHAPTER IX

MILAN AND MONTEBELLO

NAPOLEON'S rest at Milan was not of long duration. Soon after the beginning of 1797 he was obliged to take the field once more against the Austrians. In the middle of January he was again in the thick of the fight. By February 3, when Wurmser capitulated at Mantua, three Austrian armies had been destroyed in succession and all that remained was to conquer the Holy See. Josephine had been brought by her husband to Bologna before the commencement of the January campaign, and it was there that she received news from him that he expected soon to finish his task completely and to send for her. We know nothing about her stay at Bologna, but can gather from one of Napoleon's letters that she was not contented with it. "You are melancholy and ill," he said on February 16, "you no longer write to me, you want to go to Paris."

Three days afterwards he wrote again announcing that the Pope had agreed to the Treaty of Tolentino and that if her health permitted she might come to meet him at Rimini or Ravenna. " But take care of yourself, I beg you," he added. The rest of the letter is an impassioned appeal for a word from her. " What have I done ? . . . You are either ill or you do not love me. Do you think my heart is of marble ? . . . You who doubtless know too well the absolute empire which you have over me, write to me, think of me, and love me ! "

This is the last of Napoleon's letters of the Italian period preserved in Queen Hortense's collection. But the war was not yet over, as the General had hoped. Another Austrian army, led by the Archduke Charles, had entered Italy for a last effort to crush Napoleon, and he marched north again to meet it. Josephine likewise went northward and stopped at Mantua to rest. Early in March we see her writing to Hortense at Mme. Campan's to say that she was recovering from an attack of fever.

" I have been rather ill at Bologna," she continues. " Besides, I am growing weary in

Italy, in spite of all the fêtes which they give
me and the flattering welcome which I receive
from the inhabitants of this beautiful country.
I cannot accustom myself to be separated so
long from my dear children ; I want to press
them to my heart.   I have every reason, however, to hope that this moment is not very far
distant, and this helps me much to recover
from the indisposition from which I have been
suffering. . . . Write to me often.   It is very
long since I have had news from you.   Love
your mamma as she loves you, and you will
adore her.   Good-bye, my good little Hortense :
your mamma embraces you and loves you
with all her heart."

While Josephine was at Mantua, Napoleon
had driven back the Archduke and advanced
into Austrian territory.   A series of successes
brought him almost within sight of the walls
of Vienna.   An armistice was signed early in
April, followed on the 18th by the peace preliminaries at Leoben.   Then, while events were
leading up to the occupation of Venice by his
lieutenants, Napoleon rejoined Josephine.   In
May they were once more together in the com-
fortable surroundings of the Serbelloni palace

at Milan. Here, if the state had been considerable during the conqueror's previous residence, it was many times more magnificent
now. The Court of Napoleon Bonaparte had
begun, and in the midst of the combined assembly of French military notables and Italian
aristocrats Josephine forgot her desire to return
to Paris. It always pleased her in later life
to look back on this period, when the Milanese
people waited for hours to catch a glimpse of
the hero, and the hero's wife received the
homage which he delighted to see her sharing
with him. To add to her content, her son
Eugène had been called from France to join
the General's staff as aide-de-camp and lived in
the palace near her side.

The remaining days of May passed rapidly
in the midst of receptions, promenades on the
Corso, excursions to Como and Maggiore, and
all that Milan and its neighbourhood could offer.
Before the end of the month a move was made
to Montebello, about half-way between Verona
and Vicenza, which Napoleon had chosen as
his headquarters during the hot season. Here,
in a château large enough to be a palace, the
whole Bonaparte family was to be lodged and

to make at last the acquaintance of her whom
their greatest representative had introduced into
their circle without consulting them.   The
ordeal now awaited Josephine which hitherto
she had escaped.   Joseph she had met in Paris
a year before, as we have seen, and Lucien and
Louis were perhaps not quite strangers to her.
But the part which she no doubt dreaded most
still remained, to meet the Bonaparte ladies,
mother and daughters.   With what anxiety
must she not have thought of her thirty-four
years, of the complexion which required so
much rouge and powder to disguise its loss
of freshness, of the teeth whose badness she
must disguise by a smile which never opened
her lips?   And, still more, with what terror
must she not have reflected on the chances of
the betrayal by gossip of her life as a widow
in Paris and of her indiscretions since she had
by her second marriage taken the name of
those whom she was now about to encounter?

It was a rather fortunate circumstance that
Mme. Letizia Bonaparte and her daughters
did not come to Montebello entirely in the rôle
of critics.   Without waiting for the consent of
her illustrious son, the mother had but re-

cently agreed to let her eldest daughter Elisa
(Marianna) marry Felix Bacciochi, an officer
of low rank and no particular attainments,
the wedding having taken place on May 1
at Marseilles. Elisa, the least good-looking of
the Bonapartes, tall, thin, and manly rather
than womanly in appearance, had already
reached the age of twenty, which in Corsica
was considered somewhat old for an unmarried
woman, and her mother had therefore favoured
the suit of Bacciochi, who was a Corsican
himself, of Genoese origin, and remotely con-
nected with the Ramolini, Mme. Letizia's own
family. Elisa herself, although of an am-
bitious nature, was eager to be married and
saw in her suitor merits which no one else was
subsequently able to discover. One of the
principal objects of the visit to Montebello,
according to Napoleon himself,[1] was to bring
about a reconciliation over this hasty wedding.
Another was that Napoleon should conclude a
match which he had arranged for his sister
Paulette. He, who always kept so close a
watch upon the affairs of his own family, was
well aware that there was a danger of this

[1] "Mémoires," iv., 209.

reckless young girl, the spoilt beauty of the
Bonapartes, compromising herself fatally. Only
seventeen years of age, she had fallen in love
with Fréron, the Convention's Commissioner
Extraordinary in the South, where he had
proved his good republicanism by tyrannous
severity ; [1] Fréron, the man of forty, with his
retreating forehead, large nose, and prominent
eyes ; Fréron, moreover, with his family of
illegitimate children. To this man she had
written, with all that temporary intensity of
love of which she was capable : " I swear, dear
Stanislas, never to love any one but you. My
heart is shared by none ; it is given entirely
to you. Who could oppose the union of two
souls who seek only happiness and find it in
each other's love ? No, my friend, neither
mamma nor any one else can refuse you my
hand." To rescue Paulette from such an
infatuation, Napoleon was glad to give her to
his friend Victor-Emmanuel Leclerc, whom he
had first met at Toulon and had introduced to
his family after the siege. Leclerc, although

[1] It should be added, however, that Arnault describes Fréron
as not a bad man, " though he could act with violence when
stimulated by revenge or the instinct of self-preservation,"
and as an agreeable person in society.

but twenty-four, was already a general and
endeavoured strenuously to model himself on
his chief, whom he sufficiently resembled to gain
for himself later the nickname of *le Bonaparte
blond*.

Important, however, as were his sisters'
affairs, Napoleon knew as well as the others
that the really eventful feature of the gathering
at Montebello was the confronting of Josephine
and her relatives by marriage. He had made
no effort before his marriage to win over his
family, knowing that the task would have been
hopeless. He had induced Mme. Letizia and
Joseph to write to his wife in a moderately
friendly strain ; and he had endeavoured to
make Joseph and Josephine entertain amiable
feelings toward one another in Paris. He
could now only watch how the Bonaparte and
Beauharnais elements blended. It seemed at
first as if matters were going well. Mme.
Letizia, the rigid Corsican, could not be expected
to open her arms to the Creole-Parisian woman
of fashion with the damaged character. But
Josephine's careful consideration for her mother-
in-law and her air of deference conciliated
the elder woman, and there was no outward

expression of antipathy. Elisa, Paulette, and
Caroline were not more inclined to commend
their brother's choice than any other three sisters
in a similar case. Elisa, however, who had
herself a husband on probation, was gratified
that Josephine treated both her and Bacciochi
with amiability. Caroline, no more than a
child still, seems always to have agreed fairly
well with her sister-in-law until the time when,
after her marriage with Murat, she conceived
designs upon the throne of France. But between Paulette and Josephine there was an
immediate aversion. " I have never seen so
much hatred between two sisters-in-law," says
the Duchesse d'Abrantès, whose liking was no
greater for Paulette than for Josephine. It
was a case of hate at first sight, and the younger
woman soon had an opportunity of gratifying
her spite.[1]

The Leclerc-Bonaparte wedding took place
at Montebello in the middle of 1797. Arnault's
description of the bride at this period of her
life is amusing :

[1] As far as Paulette was concerned, there is no exaggeration
in saying, as M. Masson does (" Napoléon et sa Famille," i.
136), that there was a Bonaparte vendetta against the Beauharnais dating from the first day.

" If she was the prettiest creature one could
see, she was also the most unreasonable one
could imagine. She had the behaviour of a
schoolgirl, talking at random, laughing at
everything or nothing, mimicking the most
important personages, sticking out her tongue
at her sister-in-law when she was not looking,
nudging me with her knee when I did not pay
enough attention to her sallies, and drawing
upon herself from time to time those terrible
glances with which her brother called to order
the most rebellious of men. A minute later all
started over again, and the authority of the
General of the Army of Italy spent itself vainly
on a little girl's giddiness."

Her marriage with Leclerc gave Paulette an
opportunity which she welcomed of striking a
blow on her brother's behalf, as she doubtless
told herself she was doing. On Leclerc's staff,
it will be remembered, was the young hussar
Hippolyte Charles, Arnault's " good companion," the society wit and dandy. Paulette
listened with avidity to all the stories connecting
the names of Charles and Josephine and repeated
them to Napoleon. He may have heard some
of them already and of the presence of Charles

in Genoa in the previous November. That he
was at length persuaded that his earlier vague
jealousy had not been without justification
seems now certain. He took immediate action
against the hussar, but none against Josephine.
" At headquarters," says the Duchesse d'Abrantès, " the report suddenly spread that the
Commander-in-Chief had caused the arrest of
M. Charles and that he was to be shot." Instead of shooting him, however, for which he
was well aware that he could plead no military
justification, although there were also accusations against him of improper dealings with the
army contractors, Napoleon contented himself
with dismissing him from the army, thus
sparing him to tempt Josephine's fidelity again
two years later and almost to bring about a
divorce. Whether Josephine had yet justified
the suspicions against her or had been merely
indiscreet, she could not restrain her tears at
the banishment of her friend. " My sister-in-
law," said Paulette subsequently to the Duchesse
d'Abrantès in Paris, " almost died of grief, and
certainly one does not die of grief at parting
with one's friends. There must have been
more than friendship in the case. As for

MURAT.

From an engraving after a painting by Isabey.

p. 200.

me, I consoled my brother, who was very unhappy."

There is reason to think that about this time also other rumours reached Napoleon's ears, connecting his wife's name with that of Murat, who was said to have boasted of her favours at a wine-party given by him to some brother-officers of the Army of Italy.[1] Probably Napoleon had nothing definite to rely upon, but it is evident, from his subsequent behaviour during the Egyptian and Syrian expedition, that he did not forget. Nor did he forgive Murat until the time of his marriage with Caroline Bonaparte at the beginning of 1800. Whatever he may have said privately to Josephine, however, there is no hint that he gave any outward sign of bitterness against her. Some of the biographers profess to detect a change in his attitude from that of an ardent lover to that of an indulgent, but not blindly affectionate, husband ; and certainly we never see again in his correspondence with Josephine the language of overmastering passion.

In spite of the troubles arising from Jose-

---

[1] The story is, of course, to be found in the Abrantès Memoirs (ii. 238 ff.).

phine's first meeting with the ladies of her
husband's family and from his discovery that he
had not been wrong in the suggestion which he
had rather timidly ventured to make, that there
was something behind her neglect of him in his
absence—in spite of these, the three months
spent at Montebello passed, on the whole, in
pleasant fashion. Marmont may indeed be
suspected of wishing to see all in a charming
light when he writes in his Memoirs how " the
frankest and most cordial harmony reigned
among us all, and no circumstance or event ever
made any break in it." Doubtless with the
departure of the Bonapartes, not long after
Paulette's marriage to Leclerc, there came for
Josephine in particular a period of peaceful
enjoyment of the gifts of fortune. She was
still irresistible to Napoleon ; and more than
ever she was courted by those who wished to
win favour with the conqueror. Princes, towns,
the Cisalpine Republic, and the very Pope
hastened to send her presents of jewels, pictures,
other works of art and antiquities, some of which
still remain to decorate the rooms at Malmaison
which it so delighted her to fill with her trophies.
The fêtes also continued, and we hear nothing

now of the weariness with which they formerly
inspired her. In fact, her contentment with her
lot appears to have been greater than at any
time since she left Paris so unwillingly in the
previous year.

Only one blow seems to have come to lessen
her happiness—the death of Fortuné. This
little pug-dog, whom Napoleon once told
Arnault that he found in possession of madame's
bed when he married and who showed his resentment at the intruder by taking a piece out
of his leg, did not limit his hostility to men.
He met the cook's dog in the garden at Montebello, and treating him like Napoleon, found him
far from equally complacent. The result was
that Fortuné was discovered dead. "It was a
most tragic death," writes Arnault. "I leave
you to imagine what was his mistress's grief.
The conqueror of Italy could not but show his
sympathy. He mourned sincerely for an accident which left him sole possessor of his wife's
bed." But Josephine consoled herself. She
"did as many a woman does to comfort herself
for the loss of a lover ; she took another." And
Fortuné never lacked a successor during the
lifetime of Josephine.

When the three months at Montebello were over, Napoleon moved to another château in what was once Venetian territory, Passeriano, whither Josephine followed him, together with a number of ladies of her acquaintance. While Napoleon discussed with the Austrian representative the terms of the Treaty known to history as that of Campo Formio, Josephine amused herself with the society around her, and with excursions to the neighbouring places of interest, including a visit of several days' duration to Venice. When the Treaty had been signed, Napoleon left for Milan and thence, by way of Savoy and Switzerland, for Rastadt, to be present at the Congress meeting there. Josephine, who still had with her Eugène, was allowed to make her way back slowly in a kind of triumphal progress, which began at Turin and included the principal towns of Southern France, all eager to pay her the honours which they were unable at present to shower on her husband. [1]

CHAPTER X

THE UNFAITHFUL WIFE

WHILE Josephine remained in Italy in company with Eugène, Napoleon had found on his arrival at Rastadt a letter from the Directory inviting him to return to Paris at once. He hastened to comply, and on December 5, only five days after reaching Rastadt, was back in the capital, which he had not seen since he left it two days after his marriage. The eagerness of the Government and the populace to welcome the hero of Italy was great, although in the case of the Government this feeling was mixed with others which Napoleon had no difficulty in divining. The Directors entertained him on December 10 at a magnificent fête at the Luxembourg, all hung with trophies and draperies for the occasion. Before an altar to *La Patrie* sat the five Directors, to whom the victorious General was presented by Talleyrand, lately made Minister of Foreign Affairs through

the influence of Mme. de Staël. To the ex-
bishop's florid eulogy Napoleon made a brief
and brusque reply. He did not show to best
advantage at such ceremonies. Barras followed
with a speech still more ornate than Talleyrand's,
which he concluded by clasping Napoleon to
his breast. He was not the man to feel
any uneasiness over the curious bond which
existed between them in the person of
Josephine.

The Directors' entertainment, in spite of its
pomp, was quite thrown in the shade by that
given by Talleyrand, who had now no dearer
wish than to attach himself to the conqueror—
and the conqueror to him. Carnot had said of
him that, as he had already sold his calling, his
King, and his God, he would not scruple to sell
the Directory; and truly no regard for the
Directors restrained him from courting the
General whose rise threatened their safety. In
order to make the occasion additionally agreeable to Napoleon, Talleyrand waited for the
return of Josephine to Paris, which was not
until January 2, 1798, and on her arrival requested from her a list of those whom she wished
to be invited. The evening was one which was

long remembered by all who were present ;
even at Saint-Helena Napoleon recalled it with
pleasure. The Hôtel Gallifet was turned upside
down, and the host spent twelve thousand livres
on the decorations alone. Four thousand guests
passed up the grand staircase to the sound· of
music from a band placed in the cupola. Within,
the principal object was a small shrine, built
in Etruscan style, in which Talleyrand had
placed a bust of Brutus presented to him by
Bonaparte. Outside, the grounds were illuminated by Bengal lights and guarded by
soldiers drawn from all the regiments in Paris.
Talleyrand had every reason to be pleased with
the success of his arrangements. He says
himself : " The rooms in which the company
gathered had been adorned with all possible
luxury. Every one paid me compliments.
' This must have cost you a great deal, citizen
Minister,' said Mme. Merlin, wife of the Director,
to me. ' *Par le Pérou, madame,*' I answered
her in the same tone."

Napoleon and Josephine arrived at half-past
ten, she in a Greek costume, he in civilian
clothes. Arnault records that Napoleon said
to him as they entered the ball-room : " Give

me your arm. I see numbers of importunate
people waiting to attack me. While we remain
together they will not venture to break into our
conversation." Others noticed that, as far as
possible, the General kept close to his wife during
the evening, causing the remark that he was
very much in love and excessively jealous—
although, says Stanislas Girardin in his journal,
" Mme. Bonaparte is no longer pretty ; she
is nearly forty, and quite looks it."

Supper was served at midnight at a table of
three hundred covers, the women being seated,
the men standing behind them. At one o'clock
the guest of the evening and his wife withdrew.
He was not destined to escape all the " importunate people " lying in wait for him, since it
was now that the celebrated scene with Mme.
de Staël took place. The introduction was
made by Arnault, much against his wish. He
thus describes the meeting : [1]

" She overwhelmed Napoleon with compliments. He allowed the conversation to drop.
She, disappointed, searched for all possible
topics. ' General, which is the woman whom
you would love most ? ' ' My wife.' ' Very

[1] " Souvenirs," iv. 27.

simple ; but which is the one whom you would
esteem most ? ' ' The one who best knows how
to look after her household.' ' Yes, I understand. But which now would be for you the
first among women ? ' ' The one who has the
most children, madame.' "

This was all, for Napoleon turned away.
The interview was scarcely satisfactory to the
woman who had written to him that it was some
error in human institutions which had given
him as wife the sweet and tranquil Josephine,
when a soul of fire like her own was made for
the adoration of a hero like him. As she was
not wont to conceal her admirations, it is not
surprising that the story of the conversation
spread over Paris next day. Among those who
heard it with displeasure was Josephine, who
had a liking for Mme. de Staël and continued
acquaintance with her down to her last days
at Malmaison. She reproached Napoleon with
his answer, according to his own account,[1] and
told him that Paris would accuse him of
narrowmindedness (*faire le capucin*).

Life in Paris as wife of the man of the hour
was without doubt to the liking of Josephine.

[1] Quoted in Jung's " Mémoires de Lucien," ii. 235.

Everything seemed to be going well with her.[1]
She had successfully resisted the attacks made
upon her concerning her conduct in Italy by
the Bonaparte family and others. Napoleon
showed great affection for her children, and
together they watched with delight Hortense
playing her part in "Esther" at Mme. Campan's school, where she was one of the picked
pupils, just as Eugène was at the Irish College.
At home Josephine had at last in reality become
the popular hostess which some of her biographers would make her out to have been years
before. The house in the rue Chantereine was
constantly filled with the leading men and
women of the day. During her stay in Italy
she had ordered its refurnishing at a cost of more
than one hundred and twenty thousand francs.
At the end of March 1798, Napoleon bought it
for her outright, and she proceeded to put into
it the spoils of Italy, her presents from towns,

---

[1] Except, perhaps, that she was obliged to restrain her
spending impulses in the presence of Napoleon. But there were
ways of avoiding even his eye. The Duchesse d'Abrantès
remarks that, if Josephine had listened to him, " his conquest
over her prodigal spirit would have been greater than the
conquest of Egypt which he was about to undertake "
(" Mémoires," i. 424). This home conquest, however, was
one which he was never destined to make.

princes, and Pope, her statues, pictures, cameos, and antiquities, so that the house became a veritable monument of victory, most appropriate in a street which a grateful country had just renamed rue de la Victoire in compliment to her husband.

The adulation and the honours, however, which pleased Josephine wearied Napoleon. He went so far as to refuse to attend a gala performance at the Opera at which he should have been the principal guest. His inaction and dependence on others were galling to the late dictator of Italy.[1] The constant gossip about what he was going to do irritated him,

---

[1] M. Masson says (" Le Sacre et le Couronnement de Napoléon," p. 16) : " Although at times he seemed to be seeking a way of separating his fortunes from his former protectors', although he allowed some of their acts to be criticised in his presence, he was not, in spite of Campo Formio, in a position to do without them. There was no such state at the rue Chantereine as at Montebello—no princes, ambassadors, or cardinals suing for peace ; no peoples waiting on him for their independence or liberty. Certainly there were a good welcome, official eulogies, the renaming of the ' rue de la Victoire,' the rush to see him at balls, and a great popularity. But how long does that last at Paris ? Less than the fame of a singer, a courtesan, a novel, or a criminal trial. . . . So he was in a hurry to leave, just as his old friends were in a hurry to get him away. But he wanted a golden door, and this must be Egypt."

especially since much of that gossip took place in Josephine's *salon*. " All that you say," he told his wife, " is considered to come from me. Keep silence. In this way my enemies (and you are surrounded by them) will be unable to draw conclusions from your words." [1] The revival of the tale of his indebtedness to Barras, which Josephine failed to contradict, was particularly distasteful to him. For a multitude of reasons he was anxious to leave Paris. Bourrienne claims that Napoleon said to him as early as January 1798 : " Bourrienne, I don't want to stay here ; there is nothing to do. . . . I must go to the East. . . . If the success of an invasion of England appears to me doubtful, as I fear it will, the Army of England must become the Army of the East, and I shall go to Egypt."

The Army of England had been one of the topics most eagerly discussed in the salon of the rue de la Victoire. All Paris was excited about it, and it was but natural that the General's wife should be besieged by those who wished to find out what was on foot against the one Power remaining in arms out of the great coalition

[1] Duchesse d'Abrantès, i. 426.

formed in 1793 to conquer revolutionary France. Napoleon, however, on receiving the command of the new Army, did not allow himself to be led away by the ideas of others. The words which Bourrienne attributes to him may well be authentic. When it came to the point, he did not take long to reject the scheme for crossing the Channel. On February 10 he started on a tour of the northern ports from Boulogne to Dunkerque. In eight days he had seen sufficient to convince him that the idea of an invasion of England was impracticable. So, as he had said, the Army of England had to become the Army of the East. But it was essential that the plan should be kept secret, and consequently the thought of an expedition across the Channel was kept before the public as late as the end of March.

It is to the period of Napoleon's tour along the northern coast that the letter is assigned which shows Josephine to have kept up relations with Barras of which she did not wish her husband to know. This letter, undated, is addressed to "Citizen Botot, Secretary of Director Barras, at the Luxembourg" and runs :

" Bonaparte arrived to-night. Please, my dear Botot, express my regrets to Barras that I cannot come to dinner with him. Tell him not to forget me. You know better than any one else, my dear Botot, how I am placed. Good-bye. Sincere friendship.

" LAPAGERIE BONAPARTE."

This letter, it must be admitted, actually proves nothing more than that Josephine had an understanding with Barras and his secretary of which her husband was ignorant. But the wording of it and the fact that its recipient was a man disliked by Napoleon, as well as the employee of her own former protector, certainly put Josephine in a bad light. It is very unfortunate for her that one of her extremely few surviving letters, apart from those of mere affection, should be one calculated to cast grave suspicion upon her conduct at a time when otherwise she might have been believed to be paying better attention than usual to her position of wife.

The return of Napoleon to Paris, which spoilt Josephine's dinner with Barras, was the secret sign of the substitution of Egypt for England as the destination of France's attack. Nothing was allowed to leak out concerning the new plan, and Napoleon actually started for Toulon eight days in advance of his official nomination as Commander-in-Chief of the Army of the East. On the evening of May 3 he and Josephine dined with Barras at the Luxembourg and went to a performance of "Macbeth" afterwards, with Talma in the title-part. The same night they quitted Paris, Josephine still being uncertain whither they were going and leaving without having said good-bye to Hortense at Mme. Campan's.

The journey to Toulon is described by Marmont, who with Duroc, Bourrienne, and Lavalette accompanied the General and his wife in one large berlin, surmounted by a vast heap of luggage. Napoleon was in so great a hurry to reach Toulon that he ordered the driver to take a short cut, by a rough road which avoided Marseilles. It was a dark night when they entered upon this portion of the journey, and every one inside the coach was fast asleep when suddenly, during the rapid descent of a hill, a violent shock awoke all. Jumping out, they found themselves on the bank of a torrent, with a broken bridge before them. The mountain of luggage had been caught by the branch of a tree and pulled up the horses within ten feet of destruction.

It is rather strange that neither Lavalette nor Bourrienne mentions this incident in his Memoirs; nor does Josephine when writing to Hortense on May 15. Her letter merely says:

" I have been at Toulon five days, my dear Hortense; I was not at all tired by the journey, but was very vexed at leaving you so precipitately, without saying good-bye to you or my dear Caroline. But, my dear daughter, I am a little consoled for this by the hope I have of embracing you soon. Bonaparte does not wish me to embark with him; he wishes me to go to the waters before taking the journey to Egypt. He will send to fetch me in two months. . . ."

At Toulon, if she missed Hortense, Josephine found her son Eugène, who had left the Irish College of Saint-Germain to accompany his stepfather to Egypt as aide-de-camp. There also was Emilie de Beauharnais, her niece, whose marriage to Lavalette, another aide-de-camp, had been accomplished by Josephine just before leaving Paris. Emilie was the daughter of the

Vicomte Alexandre's elder brother François, and had been sent by Josephine to join Hortense at Mme. Campan's. The story was that Louis Bonaparte, on his visits to his sister Caroline's school, had seen Emilie and fallen in love with her. But Josephine, for some reason, did not wish her to marry Louis and insisted on her taking Lavalette, although there was no attraction between the two. Nevertheless it must be said for Josephine's benefit, that the match turned out well enough, whereas the extent of Louis' attachment to Emilie may be judged by the fact that when, some time later, there was a suggestion of a divorce in order that Louis might marry Mme. Lavalette, he remarked : " Even were she free, I would not marry her now. She is too much marked by smallpox." An attack of that disease had indeed greatly disfigured her after her marriage.

The Army of the East set sail from Toulon on May 19, 1798. Josephine went off to her husband's ship, the *Orient*, to bid him farewell, and then returned to land, to the balcony reserved for her and other ladies waiting to see the last of the fleet. The naval bands struck up, and the warships and forts exchanged

salutes as the expedition left the harbour.
Several vessels nearly ran aground, including
the *Orient*, but at length all got safely away.
We are told that Josephine waved a tear-wet
handkerchief to the end.

There is no reason to suppose the tears
anything but genuine, for the moment. But
Josephine's conduct throughout her husband's
stay in Egypt was such as to inspire grave doubts
as to whether her principal feeling, as she saw
the *Orient* depart, was not one of relief. She
may at first have contemplated rejoining him in
Egypt, but if she ever had any wish to do so, it
certainly faded away as the claims of society
at Plombières asserted their hold upon her.
Plombières was the watering-place which had
been selected for a visit before Napoleon's departure for Egypt. The prolongation of her
stay there was accidental. She was standing
with three friends on the wooden balcony of the
house hired by her, when the supports gave
way and precipitated all to the ground, fourteen
feet below. Josephine was rather badly hurt
and thought it necessary to summon Hortense
from school to see her. Her convalescence
lasted until August, and the solicitude of every

one about her health must have been most
flattering to her. The local authorities supplied
her daily with music and flowers, and Barras
insisted on bulletins being sent to him regularly
in Paris.

There was little inducement, perhaps, to
recover speedily. When she felt well enough
to move, Josephine went, not to Egypt, but
to Paris. This, however, was by Napoleon's
orders, for he had written to her to meet the
newly married Mme. Marmont there and to
proceed with her to Naples. Thence a ship
might convey them to Egypt by way of Malta.
The news of the battle of Aboukir, closing the
Mediterranean to all except blockade-runners,
put an end to this plan. Josephine must be
exonerated from the accusation of a refusal to
go to Egypt, in spite of what her enemies say.
The passage was well nigh impossible to all but
"Napoleon and his fortunes."

Freed from the danger of being compelled
to leave France, Josephine found herself in a
sufficiently pleasant position. Before sailing
from Toulon, Napoleon had informed her that
he had arranged that she should receive forty
thousand francs a year during his absence,

payment to be made through Joseph, in whose hands were placed all his funds. As long ago as the time when he was in Italy he had told her to look out for a suitable country house near Paris. It has been mentioned that during her visits to Croissy Josephine had seen the roofs of Malmaison, near the village of Reuil, and that she had been struck by its situation. Hither she took Napoleon on his return from Italy. He liked the house enough to offer the owner two hundred and fifty thousand francs, but in his preparations for Egypt found no time to conclude the negotiations. Josephine, however, signed a contract in her own name [1] agreeing to give two hundred and ninety thousand, including over thirty-seven thousand for the furniture. The latter was to be paid for in cash ; two hundred and ten thousand was to be owed for the present. As may be imagined, Josephine was obliged to draw upon Joseph Bonaparte for all her year's allowance in advance, and even then found a great difficulty in paying the interest on her debt.

[1] Apparently not until April 21, 1799, although she is generally made to instal herself at Malmaison soon after leaving Plombières.

The main thing, however, was that Malmaison was hers. The house was not altogether ideal. It was dilapidated and, even when repaired, somewhat resembled a barracks. It had, moreover, a reputation for unhealthiness, on which account some trace its name to a Norman *mala mansio*. But its fine position and its proximity to the Saint-Germain road appealed to Josephine; so did its grounds, laid out as a *jardin anglais* ; and so did its ample accommodation, in which she could house her treasures from Italy and the constantly accumulating additions, for which her home in the rue de la Victoire was far too small. She took up her residence at Malmaison with the greatest pleasure and began to decorate it with her statues and mosaics, her Old Masters and the rest. For new furniture, as for her dresses, jewels—already worthy of figuring in a story of the Arabian Nights, according to Mme. de Rémusat—and flowers, she could only run into further debt, since the initial expenses of Malmaison had absorbed all her cash. In July 1799 she prevailed upon the unwilling Joseph to advance her (against Napoleon's order) fifteen thousand francs for liabilities in connection with the house. It is not sur-

prising that no attempt was made to reduce the
debt of two hundred and ten thousand to the
former proprietor.

At Malmaison now Josephine proceeded to
spend most of her time, except during the cold
season. She only visited Paris for the play and
other entertainments. The winter of 1798-9
she passed in the city, however, renewing her
acquaintance with the public men, especially
the Directors Barras, Gohier, and Rewbell, to
the son of the last-named of whom she was
supposed to wish to marry Hortense. On
their side, the Directors were not at all loth to
cultivate the wife of the Commander-in-Chief
in Egypt, apart from her personal charms; for
she might at least know more than they knew
about his intentions. Josephine's *salon* in the
rue de la Victoire, therefore, was once more
thronged. But it seldom saw now within its
walls members of the Bonaparte family.
Napoleon being absent, the feud raged hotly.
Josephine's generally admired tact was unequal
to the task of conciliating the Bonapartes.
Very unwisely, heedless of the fact that they
were watching her with unremitting attention,
she both talked and acted in a way which

gave them ample opportunities to do her harm.

Mme. de Rémusat, for instance, tells of a visit which she and her mother paid to Malmaison. " Mme. Bonaparte," she says, " by nature expansive and often a little indiscreet, no sooner met my mother again than she unbosomed herself of a large number of confidences about her absent husband, her brothers-in-law, and a whole world of people who were absolute strangers to us. Bonaparte was given up as almost lost to France, his wife was neglected. My mother took pity on her, we paid her some attentions, which she never forgot."

The last two sentences show that this visit was paid in the summer of 1799. The quotation illustrates generally Josephine's lack of proper reticence when she found any one ready to be confidant of her griefs, which thus were assured of a wide audience.

But worse indiscretions than mere gossiping about her husband and his family put Josephine at the mercy of her enemies. It was probably during the winter season in Paris that she met again the Hippolyte Charles whose prospects in the army Napoleon had summarily blighted

in Italy. This re-encounter with the gay young
man nearly cost Josephine an early divorce.
It was Josephine's good nature, according to
her friends, which led her to notice Charles
again in Paris, and, by introducing him to the
Compagnie Bodin, a firm of contractors, to
endeavour to repair the damage which Napoleon
had done to his career in Italy. Charles showed
an aptitude for making money out of the Army
to which he had once belonged ; moreover, he
had experience of contractors. To express his
gratitude for her assistance he called at Malmaison. The moderate versions of the story
make him become thereafter a frequent visitor,
who stopped late strolling in the park at Malmaison with his hostess. As only a ditch
separated the park from the road to Saint-
Germain, passers-by could see them in the moon-
light, Josephine in her white dress and scarf,
Charles in his black or blue clothes. The
villagers, ignorant of the facts, told how the
lady loved "her brother." Others, better informed, had a different tale to tell. Laurette
Permon was acquainted with what was going
on through a friend of her mother, and she felt
no doubt as to Josephine's guilt. She writes

in her Memoirs [1] that " M. Charles lived at Malmaison quite as if he were its master. Friends have their privileges."

Josephine of course must have been well aware what a weapon against her the scandal about Charles would prove in the hands of the Bonapartes ; and she did not altogether neglect to provide herself with friends whose respectability was unimpeachable, in order that she might call them as witnesses to character. In particular she cultivated the society of Gohier, the President of the Directory, and his wife, against whom no one could bring any complaint on the score of morals at least ; for Gohier had married his cook. To this eminently trustworthy household Josephine paid more and more visits as time went on. Now Gohier was not unaware of the stories in circulation about Josephine, and, according to the Duchesse d'Abrantès, after failing to persuade her that she ought to break off all relations with Charles, advised her to work for a divorce. " You tell me that you and M. Charles feel nothing but friendship for one another," he is represented as saying. " But if this friendship is so exclusive

[1] Duchesse d'Abrantès, " Mémoires," iii. 207-10.

of all else that it makes you fly in the face of
convention, I must tell you the same as if it
were a case of love : Get a divorce ! ''

If this speech of Gohier's is truly reported,
Josephine's position must indeed have been
desperate. She had other reasons for thinking
so, too, besides Gohier's warning. One evening
she went into Paris from Malmaison to a dinner
given by Barras at the Luxembourg. The
guests included the Talliens and Talleyrand,
and the last-named sat between Josephine and
Mme. Tallien. Less than two years ago the
Minister of Foreign Affairs had been at Josephine's feet, nor had he neglected to pay her
court since then. But this evening he gave no
attention to her and devoted all his time to
his other neighbour. So marked was his conduct
that at length Josephine rose from the table,
went into another room, and wept. What
could be the explanation of Talleyrand's behaviour ? Since it could hardly be that he had
received early private intelligence of Napoleon's
death in Egypt, it must be that he had news
of a determination to divorce Josephine. Only
if he were certain of her approaching disgrace
could he dare to treat her as he did this night

at the Luxembourg. But it was too late to do anything. There was but one chance, to see Napoleon as soon as he returned, before any one else could get to him. " If only I am the first to see him, he will throw himself into my arms." Such are the words attributed to her when she knew that he was in France. His arrival must have been at once dreaded by her and recognised as her only hope.

There was not long to wait now for the critical moment. On the evening of October 10 she was at the Luxembourg again, dining this time with Gohier and his wife. Suddenly the news came to the President of the Directory that Napoleon had landed on the previous night at Fréjus in Provence. It was a moment to make all feel anxious. Josephine, striving to hide all personal emotion, addressed herself to Gohier. " President, do not be afraid that Bonaparte comes with intentions hostile to liberty. But you must unite to prevent him falling into bad hands. I am going to meet him. It is important for me not to be anticipated by his brothers, who have always detested me." It is Gohier himelf who reports this speech, in his Memoirs. Josephine then looked at Mme.

Gohier, he says, and added: "However, I have nothing to fear from calumny. When Bonaparte learns that my favourite society has been with you he will be as flattered as he will be grateful for the welcome which I have had in your house during his absence."

This was certainly putting on a brave face, but her listeners can hardly have been deceived into crediting Josephine with the confidence which she professed. In the eyes of all who had watched the drama it must have appeared that the curtain was about to go up on the final scene, when the sinning wife was to pay for the offences which she had committed against so fond and forgiving a husband. The scene was indeed a final one, but not of the drama of the married life of Josephine and Napoleon. It was final, to our knowledge, as far as the story of Josephine's unfaithfulness is concerned. With regard to her life as wife to Napoleon, however, it may be said to be only the end of the introductory act.

NAPOLEON BONAPARTE.

From an engraving after the picture by J. Guérin

p. 228.

CHAPTER XI

IN order to understand what was the position of affairs when Josephine and Napoleon met in October 1799, it is necessary to go back to the summer of the previous year, when Josephine was still at Plombières recovering from her accident. In August 1798 a French vessel was captured at the mouth of the Nile by English warships. Among the correspondence on board was found a letter dated July 25 and written by Napoleon to his brother Joseph. The latter, of course, never received it, but part of it was printed in the English papers. The most important sentences, as far as we are concerned, are as follows:

" I may be in France within two months. I commend my affairs to you. I have great domestic trouble, for the veil has been entirely removed. . . . It is a sad state of affairs to have at the same time all kinds of feelings in

the same heart toward one and the same person
—you understand what I mean. See that I
have a country house on my arrival, either near
Paris or in Burgundy. I expect to pass the
winter there and to shut myself up. I am tired
of human nature. I have need of solitude
and isolation. Greatness wearies me, feeling is
dried up, glory is unmeaning. . . . I mean to
keep my house. I will never give it up to any
one, whoever it may be.''

From this letter it is plain that as early as
the July after he had left Toulon Napoleon contemplated a separation from Josephine ; since
for no other reason could he require a new
country house, when Josephine had already
bought Malmaison, nor would he have announced his determination not to give up to
any one the house in the rue de la Victoire, which
he had taken over from Josephine. By whom
then had the veil been " entirely removed "
since he left France ? Not by Joseph, for there
would in that case have been some indication
of the fact in Napoleon's letter. It has been
suggested that during the voyage from Toulon
to Alexandria Napoleon had questioned some
of his old comrades of the Army of Italy and

had been enlightened by them with regard to
the relations between Josephine and Charles—
and perhaps Murat also. M. Masson has, however, published[1] a letter written by Eugène to
his mother, dated one day previous to the
above quoted letter from Napoleon to Joseph.
The boy says herein :

" Bonaparte for five days seemed very melancholy, and this followed after a talk which he had
with Julien, Junot, and also Berthier. He was
more affected than I should have believed by
these conversations. All that I heard amounted
to this, that Charles came in your carriage to
within three post-stations of Paris, that you
have seen him in Paris, that you have been to
the fourth tier of the Italiens with him, that
he gave you your little dog, and that he is even
at this moment with you. This is all that I
could overhear, in broken words. You know
quite well, mamma, that I do not believe this,
but what is certain is that the General is much
affected. Nevertheless he has redoubled his
kindness to me. He seems by his actions to
wish to say that the children are not answerable
for the faults of their mother. But your son

[1] " Joséphine répudiée," 17–18.

chooses to think all this gossip the invention of your enemies. He does not love you the less for it, nor desire the less to embrace you. I hope when you come all will be forgotten. . . ."

This passage in Eugène's letter certainly sheds light on a difficult question, although it does not reveal how the scandal about Josephine and Charles reached Egypt. Whatever the ultimate source of his information, Napoleon seems to have been temporarily calmed by extreme pressure of work, for we hear of no further outbreak until we come to the date of the celebrated conversation with Junot at the springs of the Messoudiah on February 17, 1799. It seems clear that in February Napoleon received some news from Paris which aroused him to fury, whether it related to past affairs or to Josephine's continued acquaintance with Charles.[1]

The scene at the Messoudiah springs is described by Bourrienne, whose account perhaps deserves more belief than many of his stories, in that, although he is always a witness

[1] Bourrienne says that, though Bonaparte did not tell him, he had " plenty of reasons for thinking that Murat's name had been coupled with that of Charles in the indiscretions of Junot at the source of the Messoudiah."

most friendly to Josephine, what he here
narrates puts her in an unfavourable light.

"I saw Bonaparte," writes Bourrienne,
"walking alone with Junot, as often happened.
I was a little distance away, and I do not
know why my eyes were fixed on him during
this conversation. The always pale face of
the General had become even paler than usual,
without my being able to guess the reason.
There was something convulsive about it,
something wild in his looks, and several times
he struck his head. After a quarter of an
hour's talk he left Junot and came back toward
me. I had never seen him with so discontented
and preoccupied an air. I went forward to
meet him, and as soon as we were together he
said to me in a brusque, hard tone : ' You don't
care for me at all. . . . These women ! Josephine ! . . . If you had cared for me, you would
have told me all that I have just learnt from
Junot. He is a true friend. Josephine ! . . .
and I am six hundred leagues away. You
ought to have told me. Josephine ! . . . To
think that she should have deceived me so ! . . .
She ! . . . Curse them ! I will wipe out this
race of fops and coxcombs. As for her,

divorce ! . . . Yes, divorce, a public and sensational divorce ! . . . I must write ! I know everything. . . . It is your fault. You ought to have told me about it."

The secretary tried to calm his General and to persuade him not to listen to jealous slanders. It was necessary, he said, to avoid such a scandal in his position. When he spoke, however, of Napoleon's future and of his glory, Napoleon broke in : " My glory ? Oh, I don't know what I would give not to have what Junot told me true, I love this woman so ! If Josephine is guilty, I must have a divorce to separate us for ever. I don't want to be the laughing-stock of all the idlers of Paris. I shall write to Joseph. He will get a divorce for me."

The Duchesse d'Abrantès denies the truth of Bourrienne's account. But she was Junot's wife and would naturally not wish him to appear as the accuser of his future Empress. It is certain that Josephine never afterwards had a friendly feeling for either Junot or his wife—the latter of whom has taken a voluminous revenge in her Memoirs.

An independent, though naturally not un-

PRINCE EUGÈNE DE BEAUHARNAIS.

From a painting at Versailles.   Photo by Neurdin Frères.

biassed, witness to Napoleon's trouble of mind
at this period is Eugène de Beauharnais. The
seventeen-year-old aide-de-camp found himself
in a very unpleasant position while his step-
father was receiving the damaging accusations
against his mother. Eugène says in his
Memoirs :

" Although I was very young, I inspired
him with sufficient confidence in me to cause
him to reveal his trouble to me. It was
usually in the evening that he made his complaints and confidences to me, taking long
strides up and down his tent. I was the only
one to whom he could unbosom himself freely.
I tried to soften his resentment and consoled
him as best I could and as much as my age
and the respect I felt for him allowed me."

Eugène's difficulty became greater still when,
in his disgust at his betrayal, and after his
return from Syria to Egypt, Napoleon took
up Mme. Fourès, wife of an officer in the
chasseurs.[1] So public was this affair—his first

----

[1] Bourrienne says it was in *September 1798* that Napoleon
" fell violently in love with Mme. Fourès, the wife of an
infantry lieutenant. She was very pretty, and her charms
were enhanced by the rarity in Egypt of women calculated to
please European eyes. Bonaparte took for her a house

infidelity to Josephine since their marriage—
that "Our Lady of the East" became a
commonplace in the mouths of the Army in
Egypt. Naturally relations were now strained
between Eugène and his step-father. Eugène
writes guardedly :

" General Bonaparte paid some attention to
a certain officer's wife and sometimes drove
out with her. People did not fail to say she
was his mistress, so that my position, both as
aide-de-camp and as son of the General's wife,
grew painful. Forced by my duties to accompany the General, who never went out
without his aide-de-camp, I had already allowed
myself to accompany the carriage once when,
unable to bear the humiliation any longer, I
sought out General Berthier and asked him
for permission to join a regiment. This step
was followed by a sharp scene between my
step-father and myself, but he ceased from
this moment to take his rides with the lady.

adjoining Elfy Bey's palace, which we occupied. He frequently
ordered dinner to be prepared there, and I used to go with
him at seven o'clock and to leave him at nine. The connection
soon became the general subject of gossip at headquarters."
Napoleon, he adds, sent Fourès home on a mission to the
Directory, but the English captured him and maliciously sent
him back to Egypt.

I remained with him, and he treated me none the worse for what had happened."

Eugène Beauharnais was loyal to his patron, as well as a dutiful and affectionate son, and he has minimised the extent of Napoleon's intrigue with Mme. Fourès. With regard to his mother, he probably felt that he could more easily love than excuse her. He admits that when, having decided to return to France, Napoleon came to him and said : "Eugène, you are going to see your mother again," his joy was not as great as it ought to have been.

Leaving Egypt on the night of August 22-3, and breaking their voyage in Corsica, Napoleon and Eugène landed at Fréjus on October 9, having successfully escaped the English cruisers in the Mediterranean. The journey from Fréjus to Aix was made by night along a road lighted by the torches of an enthusiastic crowd. At Avignon, Valence, and Lyon the welcome was equally warm for the expected deliverer of France from over-taxation, anarchy, and internal revolt. One day's halt was made at Lyon, during which time Napoleon could not stir without the attentions of a wildly applauding mob. The fears of the Directory concerning

his return were amply justified in the first
hours spent by Napoleon in France.

There were other eyes, however, as anxious
in their way as the Directors', watching for
Napoleon's arrival. And not all the watchers
were content to wait. Josephine on the
morning after the Gohiers' dinner started
off to Lyon; so did his brothers Joseph,
Lucien, and Louis, and his brother-in-law
and friend Leclerc — Josephine with the
thought, "If only I am the first to see
him he will throw himself into my arms,"
the brothers burning with zeal to anticipate
her. Now it happened, unfortunately for
Josephine, that it was possible for Napoleon
to proceed from Lyon to Paris by either of
two ways. He actually chose the Bourbonnais
route, and taking only Eugène with him,
hastened in a light carriage toward Paris. On
the way he met Joseph, Lucien, and Leclerc,
Louis having fallen ill and remained behind.
Josephine, knowing Napoleon's affection for
the Burgundian country, had taken the other
road and arrived at Lyon to find him gone.
An immediate return brought her to Paris
again forty-eight hours after Napoleon, and at

least three days after his meeting with his brothers. They had had full time to do their worst, and Josephine might well despair.

The great desire of the Bonapartes, the end for which they had been observing their sister-in-law's conduct for so long, was that they should get hold of Napoleon and persuade him, before he reached Paris, that he must put his wife away at once. They saw the *coup d'État* coming which might put their brother at the head of the Government. Josephine must not be allowed, even for a day, to share with Napoleon the first place. All had fallen out well for them. They poured their complaints— his wrongs—into his ears, and when he arrived at the rue de la Victoire he knew the worst that they could say about her. Possibly he intended to give her a hearing before coming to any decision. When he reached his house, however, he found all his own family there, but no Josephine. Was she ill ? he demanded. The only answer was a smile, than which nothing could suggest worse. The shock was terrible and profound, says the Duchesse d'Abrantès, who claims to be well acquainted with all that was passing. " He thought that,

as he did not find her in the midst of his
family, supported by his sisters, presented by
his mother, she felt herself unworthy of their
protection and was flying the very presence of
him whom she had dishonoured. The mistake about the roads seemed to him a mere
excuse."

Josephine was not left entirely unbefriended,
though the advocate who appeared could only
use arguments like those of Bourrienne at the
Messoudiah springs. An acquaintance of both
husband and wife, Collot, came to the rue de
la Victoire. " There will be nothing in future
between her and me," declared Napoleon.
" What, are you going to leave her ? " " Has
she not deserved it ? " " I do not know, but
is this the time to think about it ? " asked
Collot, who begged him to remember that
France's eyes were upon him and would only
see in him, if he engaged in domestic quarrels
now, " one of Molière's husbands." Napoleon
listened to the end and then only said that
Josephine should never set foot in his house,
but must go to Malmaison. The public knew
too much to make any mistake about the
reasons for her departure. Collot told him

that his very violence proved that he was still in love. " She will come and make her excuses, you will forgive her, and all will be peace." " I forgive her ? Never ! " cried the irritated Napoleon. " How little you know me ! If I were not sure of myself I would tear my heart out and throw it on the fire." He stopped, almost choked with his vehemence, and put his hand to his breast as if he meant to fulfil his threat.

But the celebrated scene was at hand which has left the greatest impression on the popular imagination in connection with the story of Napoleon and Josephine. Josephine arrived by night from her futile journey to Lyon, and entered the house in the rue de la Victoire. Napoleon was locked up in his private study and refused absolutely to see her. He walked up and down the room with long strides, furiously angry and declaring that he had been too kind to her in Italy, but now he would never see her again, never ! Outside stood Josephine knocking at the door, weeping and dishevelled, crying : " Open the door, *mon ami, mon bon ami*, I will explain everything. . . . Oh, he won't open it ! . . . What have you against me, tell me ? . . . Oh, if you knew all the harm you are doing me ! "

Napoleon took no apparent notice of her sobs and cries. Easily moved as he usually was by tears, on this occasion he could not see them and had the strength to resist them. In her desperation she rolled upon the floor and struck her head against the door. At length an idea came to her. There were her children, for whom he had always shown an affection rare in a step-father, and whom he had seemed to love as being part of his wife. Could he turn them away now, along with her ? Eugène and Hortense came at their mother's bidding. Napoleon did not refuse to see them, and they entered his room.

" Bonaparte was reduced to silence," says the Duchesse d'Abrantès, who describes the events with extreme minuteness, " and could offer no opposition to the irresistible appeal of two young and innocent creatures kneeling at his knees, bathing his hands with their tears, and each repeating : ' Don't abandon my mother, it will kill her. And must we poor orphans, whose natural guardian has already been torn from us by the scaffold, must we unjustly be robbed of the guardian whom Providence sent us ? ' "

The struggle was over. " Go and fetch your mother," said the man who had declared himself inflexible. Josephine was lying on the stairs outside his room. She was lifted up and brought in. She fell into his arms without a word, though not without a tear, and then probably fainted—which was better diplomacy than the promised explanation. Napoleon raised her and carried her to his bed. Perhaps she explained all then. At any rate, at seven next morning Lucien Bonaparte received a summons to come to the rue de la Victoire and was ushered into a room where he found his brother and his sister-in-law still in bed. Nothing could have shown him so briefly that the schemes against Josephine had failed.

Josephine could hardly have hoped for an easier victory, after the Bonaparte family had beaten her so decidedly in the race to reach Napoleon first. Still, her anguish outside the door, the genuineness of which it is impossible to doubt, was not without its permanent effect upon her. This night seems to have been the turning-point of her life, in one respect. We do not again hear of her wifely unfaithfulness. She was still the old Josephine who concealed her extravagant debts from her husband, above all men, and made a confidant of almost any one before him, but she no longer betrayed him with a Barras, a Murat, or a Charles. Her narrow escape from a shameful divorce had shown her that she had trusted almost too much in the forgiveness which had not failed her before ; and her amendment of her ways, in this particular, appears to have been complete.

The generosity of Napoleon was decidedly remarkable. He only stipulated that Josephine should never again see Hippolyte Charles, who thereupon passes out of the history in which he played so small and ignoble a part. But Napoleon never forgot his hatred of him, and no one ever ventured to mention the name of Hippolyte Charles in his presence again. One day, long after, the Emperor was walking arm in arm with Duroc to see the Austerlitz Bridge just then in the course of construction. A cab passed them in the street, and Duroc felt the weight on his arm suddenly grow heavy. He turned and saw Napoleon looking pale and

faint. " What is it ? " he cried in alarm.
" Nothing," said Napoleon peremptorily, " be
quiet ! " The occupant of the cab was Charles.

With regard to Murat, there is no evidence
that Napoleon said anything to Josephine now,
but it was evident later that his indiscretion,
whatever it amounted to, was not forgotten
either. The only bitter comment on the situation which we find attributed to Napoleon
is his remark to Réal : " The warriors from
Egypt are like those from the siege of Troy,
and their wives have been equally faithful."

Bourrienne adds a paragraph to the story
of the reconciliation which is interesting if true.
Collot, Josephine's advocate of a day or two
before, was invited to breakfast on the morning
after all was over. " Well, she is here," said Napoleon to him as soon as they were alone. He
went on to explain how he had come to break
his resolve. " As she went downstairs weeping,
I saw Eugène and Hortense following her with
tears. I have not the kind of heart which can
bear to see tears flowing. Eugène was with
me in Egypt and I have been accustomed to
look on him as my adopted son. He is a brave
and good boy. Hortense is just about to come

out into the world. All who know her speak well of her to me. I confess, Collot, that I was deeply moved. I could not resist the sobs of these two poor children. I asked myself, Ought they to be victims of the faults of their mother ? I kept Eugène, Hortense fetched her mother. What could I do ? One can't be a man without being weak." " You may be sure they will repay you," said Collot. " They ought to, Collot, they ought to, for it has cost me dear enough."

There were others, of course, affected by the reconciliation beside the two principals and the Beauharnais children. The Bonaparte brothers, especially Joseph and Lucien, would have found it hard to conceal their vexation at the failure which had befallen them when everything seemed to promise success ; but there were the great events of *brumaire* to prepare for, and it was necessary to patch up a domestic truce in order to devote all energies to public affairs. Of the women of the family, although Josephine had not a friend in one of them, none openly displayed any displeasure at what had happened except Paulette (Mme. Leclerc) ; and she was so much in the habit of

speaking her mind on all occasions that little
attention was paid to her.   Mme. Letizia, however, could not altogether conceal her feelings,
little though she was wont to talk unguardedly.
Speaking to her old friend Mme. Permon, who
asked her why she did not go to the rue de la
Victoire for some information which she wanted,
she said : " Signora Panoria, I do not go there
to satisfy my heart, but to Julie's or Christine's.
There I see my sons happy.   As for the other
one . . . no, no ! " So saying she tightened
her lips and opened her eyes, as was characteristic of her when deeply interested in what she
was talking about.[1]   There could be no doubt
that she regretted that Napoleon had not
repudiated his wife.

[1] Duchesse d'Abrantès, "Mémoires," ii. 127.

CHAPTER XII

A S soon as she had obtained forgiveness for her infidelity during 1798-9, Josephine was given a part to play in the preparations for the *coup d'État* which is surprisingly large in view of what we know of Napoleon's detestation of the interference of women in politics. As late as the time of his return from Italy, he had forbidden his wife to talk of public affairs " since she knew nothing about them." But now he felt the need of a certain help which she, and no one else, was able to give him. He was himself out of touch with the society of the period. His family could aid him little here. Joseph and Lucien, although they had undoubtedly been playing for their own hands rather than for his, had influence with the Councils, the elder as a lobbyist, the younger as an orator ; but they could not influence sections of the great world of Paris on whom

it was imperative for Napoleon to have a hold.
Josephine, however, could do so. Seldom as
she may have thought of her absent husband
in Egypt, she had maintained connections which
were capable of being used for his great advantage after his return to Paris. The love
which she manifested, throughout life, of a
" pull " with those in authority was at the
present moment of the utmost service to the
man whom she had wronged. Gohier, Rewbell,
and, of course, Barras were her friends among
the Directors. The Directory which, in Napoleon's own words, trembled at his home-
coming was most amiable to the wife of him
whom they feared. Then, again, Josephine's
liking for the old aristocracy and the leaders
of fashion was also useful. Her talent for
cajolery had a full opportunity for display, and
that talent was very real. She was very different
now from the young girl whom the Vicomte de
Beauharnais had despaired of being able to
teach. She had learnt to be a graceful and
attractive hostess.

A picture drawn by Arnault of one of the
evenings in the rue de la Victoire illustrates
this better than any other description could.

" Josephine," writes Arnault, " did the honours of her *salon* more gracefully than ever. There might be seen there men of every party, generals, deputies, Royalists, Jacobins, abbés, a Minister, and even the President of the Directory. To judge by the air of superiority of the master of the house, one might have thought him already a monarch amid his court." On the night in question, Fouché, the Minister of Police, arrives late, and as he seats himself by Josephine is asked by Gohier for the latest news. Fouché speaks of the rumours of conspiracy, and after begging them to trust him to deal with it, bursts into a laugh. How can he laugh at such things ? asks Josephine. Gohier (who is not in the conspiracy) reassures her : " Be easy, citizeness ; when a man talks of such things before ladies, it is because he does not think that he will have to act. Be like the Government—don't worry yourself about these rumours. Sleep in peace ! "

Near at hand stood Napoleon, listening with a smile. It was on the eve of the contemplated upset of the Government by the conspiracy of which Gohier knew so little and the others so much.

The stroke had been planned for the 16 *brumaire an VIII*. (November 7, 1799); but a postponement was made for two days. As President of the Directory, Gohier was meanwhile the object of the politest attentions from Bonaparte and his wife. While the husband told Gohier that it would give him great pleasure to dine with him on the 18th, the wife had a still more important task entrusted to her— nothing less than an attempt to force the President into joining the attack on the Government. It had been arranged that at six in the morning of the 18 *brumaire*, the officers of the army in Paris and the National Guard should meet at Napoleon's house. At midnight on the 17th Josephine sent Eugène to the Luxembourg with an invitation for Gohier and his wife to breakfast with her next morning. " Do not fail to come," she wrote. " I have some very interesting matters to talk about to you." Gohier in his Memoirs says that the hour mentioned by " the good Josephine " seemed to him suspicious. He therefore told his wife to go alone and to tell her hostess that he would have the honour of calling later. She arrived at the appointed hour and found the

house full of officers. Napoleon greeted her
with the remark that Gohier must come. Would
she write to tell him so ? Mme. Gohier wrote,
sending the note by her own servant. But
what she said to her husband was that he had
done right in staying away, as everything
pointed to a trap. When the message had
gone, Josephine came up to her and said :
" What you notice must make you foresee the
inevitable. I cannot tell you how grieved I
am that Gohier has not accepted my invitation. I planned it with Bonaparte, who wants
the President of the Directory to be one of
the members of the Government which he pro-
poses to set up. When I sent the letter by
my son's hands, it ought to have shown him
what importance I attached to it."

Mme. Gohier insisted that she must go back
to her husband, as she was not wanted where
she was. Josephine would not detain her, but
begged her, as she left, to use all her influence
to win her husband to join them. " I must
warn you," she said at parting, " that at this
moment Talleyrand and Bruix are with Barras,
asking him to resign, which he will doubtless
not refuse to do. Besides, they are authorised

to tell him that Bonaparte is quite determined to use all means, even force, if he ventures to make the slightest resistance." Even after the wife's departure she did not abandon all hope of persuading the husband, but sent to him a joint friend of theirs to let him know that if he merely refrained from opposing the conspirators he should have the Ministry of Justice in the new Government. Gohier takes some pride in his refusal of this offer ; but, though he wrote a letter (intercepted by Napoleon) denouncing the plot to the Five Hundred, he became reconciled later, and in two years' time accepted the post of Consul-General in Holland.

Josephine's exertions to win over the Gohiers seem to prove her gratitude to her respectable friends, who she had once thought might justify her conduct in Napoleon's eyes. The story also shows her entrusted with a task of no little importance in the conspiracy of *brumaire*. For the remainder of the two days during which Napoleon established his hold on the leading place in the Republic she had little to do but wait and watch. On the 19th, between nine and ten at night, Mme. Letizia

Bonaparte and her daughters arrived at the rue de la Victoire to obtain certain news of the alleged attempt on Napoleon's life at Saint-Cloud. They had been at the theatre when the report reached them. In her anxiety, Mme. Bonaparte had put aside her scruples and consented to go to her daughter-in-law. It would be interesting had we any description from eye-witnesses of Josephine's reception of her visitors ; but there is none. On that day all attention was turned to Napoleon, and his wife remains in the background. It was between three and four the next morning when the new Consul, accompanied in a carriage by his colleague Sieyès, his brother Lucien, and General Gardanne, drove over from Saint-Cloud. His arrival at the rue de la Victoire is left to the imagination, and no pen has told how Josephine received the news that she was wife of the Dictator of France.

On the day following the overthrow of the former Government, Napoleon and Josephine moved from their private house to the Petit-Luxembourg. It was necessary that a few weeks should pass before Napoleon, as First Consul by general consent, should occupy the

Tuileries. The supersession of the politicians
by the military hero was not yet complete.
The hero's assistants, without whom he would
have fared so ill on the 18 and 19 *brumaire*,
had susceptibilities, and could not have seen
without protest all the power falling at once
into the hands of one man, whoever he might
be. The state observed at the Petit-Luxembourg, therefore, was modest. Napoleon had
rooms on the ground floor, a private staircase
from his study leading to the first floor, where
Josephine and her daughter were lodged. There
was no luxury at the table. The ten o'clock
breakfast and five o'clock dinner were both
short meals. After the latter, Napoleon went
upstairs to Josephine's apartments, where receptions were held nightly. But at midnight,
at the latest, Napoleon's brusque " *Allons nous
coucher!* " was a sign for breaking up, and
the day was over.

The evening receptions alone showed the
slightest departure from Republican and bour-
geois simplicity, and even they were not much
more formal, perhaps, than the Directors'
salons had been. Only the manners were
better, and it is recorded that now for the

first time since the Revolution the title " Madame " began to be heard again, to the disgust of many uncompromising citizens. The Petit-Luxembourg was the resort of society, political, artistic, and fashionable ; and at last Josephine was society's leader, supplying by her tact and amiability the many deficiencies of her husband, whether they were caused by ill-humour, absorption in work, or natural temperament. The better section of her personal friends, the remnants of the ex-nobles and the *ralliés*, came to blend as far as possible with the new blood. The times forbade a too close scrutiny into character, but admittance by card of invitation only preserved the *salon* from the intrusion of some of the more disreputable frequenters of the Directory entertainments. There was a certain restraint which had been decidedly lacking before. Like his nephew later, after the establishment of the Second Empire, Napoleon Bonaparte insisted particularly on the observance of decorum among the ladies who came to his receptions. He had his theories as to what was proper in their dress. An amusing story is preserved in the " Moniteur " of the period. There was

CAROLINE BONAPARTE (MURAT).

After an etching by Flaning.

p 256.

a large party gathered at the Luxembourg,
and, it being December still, the fires were
alight. Suddenly the Consul ordered the fire
to be made up. He was obeyed, but still repeated his command two or three times. At
last one of the servants pointed out that there
was no room for any more fuel. Napoleon
raised his voice and said : " That will do. I
wanted a good fire to be made up, for the cold
is intense. Besides, these ladies are nearly
naked." After the eccentricities of the Directory period, when it was not considered out-
rageous to appear in the costume of Diana
in the open air, such a remark must have occasioned a considerable shock.

While the Bonapartes were still at the Luxembourg, a marriage took place in the family
which was attributed to Josephine's instigation ;
namely, that of Murat and Caroline, sister of
Napoleon. In view of the scandal involving
herself and the handsome Murat in the past,
Josephine may have been glad of the opportunity to show her husband that she only
wished the young soldier well, and had no sort
of personal attachment to him. If so, she
seems to have produced the right effect, for

Bourrienne states that Napoleon said to him :
" I am rejoiced that my wife is interested in
this match.   You can easily guess the reasons."
Murat and Caroline, however, needed no prompt-
ing.   The former had met his General's sister
at Montebello, and again in Paris after the
return from Egypt.[1] Caroline and Hortense
were spending their holidays at the rue de la
Victoire ; to get them out of the way of the
conspiracy, both were sent back to Mme.
Campan's academy before *brumaire*.   The story
goes that Murat was thoughtful enough on
the night of the 19th to send four of his grena-
diers to Saint-Germain to give Caroline the
news of her brother's success.   As it was very
late when they arrived at the school, it is
probable that Mme. Campan appreciated the
attention less than her pupil.

In spite of the mutual attachment of the two,
Napoleon did not welcome the idea of a marriage at first.   He expressed his disapproval of
ces mariages d'amourettes.   It was suspected that
he designed his sister for General Moreau, while

---

[1] The Duchesse d'Abrantès says that Caroline " loved Murat
passionately," and that Murat was very much in love with
her (ii. 241).

he had looked on Murat ever since the Italian
days with a dislike which not even his extreme
bravery at Aboukir or his much-needed support
in the Council of the Five Hundred on the 19
brumaire had been able to remove. When,
therefore, Murat asked him for Caroline's hand,
he merely replied that he would think about
the proposal. The same evening he mentioned
the subject to Josephine in the presence of
her two children and of Bourrienne. Josephine
at once supported Murat's suit, and the others
when appealed to agreed with her. Napoleon's
objections were met by references to Aboukir
and *brumaire*. " I admit that Murat was
splendid at Aboukir," he replied, and at length
he gave way. After all, he told Bourrienne
such a marriage would please the Republicans
better than a noble alliance for Caroline. It
could not be forgotten that Murat was an inn-
keeper's son.

Accordingly the match was made, and on
January 18, 1800, the contract was signed, the
civil marriage taking place at Joseph's house at
Mortefontaine two days later. The couple appeared well suited. Murat was one of the best-
looking men in the army and had a reputation

for quite reckless courage. Caroline, although she was not the peer of her sister Paulette, was universally admired. At eighteen she is described as having a dazzling complexion and a beautiful skin, with a pleasing and ingenuous expression. She had, however, a decision of character contrasting with the childish gracefulness of her face. She appreciated her husband's many weak points; she also had a better understanding than the rest of her family of the strength and weakness of her celebrated brother, whom she was said to resemble more than the others.

In connection with this Murat-Bonaparte marriage, there is told one of the many stories of Josephine's passion for jewellery, which is at the same time illustrative of her readiness to deceive her husband, no matter who her fellow-conspirators might be. Napoleon treated his sister very generously in the marriage settlement, giving her a dowry of thirty thousand francs. He also wished to make her a wedding present of value and, apparently not having sufficient funds immediately at hand, selected from among his wife's jewels a diamond collar, which he presented to Caroline. Josephine was not unnaturally grieved over the loss of her collar. She knew that the jeweller Foncier had a collection of pearls, said to have been the property of Marie Antoinette. She thought that if she could acquire these she would be consoled. But Foncier asked a sum for them variously stated at two hundred and fifty and five hundred and fifty thousand francs. She could not allow such a bill to fall into Napoleon's hands, nor could she pay it unaided. Accordingly she appealed to Berthier, the Minister of War, who was well disposed to her and not scrupulous. It happened that he wished to have admitted to the Luxembourg his mistress, Mme. Visconti. If this could be done, he would divert in Josephine's favour a sum of money intended for hospital expenses for the French Army in Italy. The compact was made, and it only remained for Josephine to explain the presence of the pearls, since Napoleon had an attentive eye for her wardrobe. There was no difficulty, however, in finding another friend as accommodating as Berthier. Bourrienne is himself witness to his own treachery toward his patron.[1] One day Josephine said to him : " Bourriénne,

[1] " Mémoires," iii. 293.

there is a large party to-morrow, I must wear
my pearls. But you know *him*. He is sure to
scold if he notices. Please don't go away,
Bourrienne ; if he asks me where my pearls
come from, I shall tell him without hesitation
that I have had them a long time." Bourrienne
agreed to stand by her. Next evening Napoleon
came up and said to Josephine : " Ah, what
have you got there ? How fine you look to-
day ! What are those pearls ? I do not seem
to have seen them on you before." " Good
Heavens ! That is the collar which the Cisalpine Republic gave to me. I have put it
in my hair." " But I seem . . ." " Well,
ask Bourrienne, he will tell you." " What do
you say, Bourrienne ? " asked Napoleon. " Do
you recall them ? " " Yes, General," was the
strictly truthful answer, " I well remember
having seen them before."

In spite of the pain which the loss of her
diamond collar caused to Josephine until she
had replaced it, it does not appear that she felt
any grudge against Caroline as the recipient
of her jewellery. Of the three Bonaparte sisters
Caroline was the one with whom she was on
the best terms. After her marriage she accom-

panied Josephine and Hortense both in Paris and to Malmaison ; and a letter remains, written by Josephine to Murat on June 20, 1800, which runs as follows :

" I have only just time, dear little brother, to recommend to you the bearer of my letter, to assure you of my fond attachment and to tell you that you have a charming little wife, who behaves admirably.   Good-bye, dear little brother, I embrace you and love you well."

This curious note might almost be taken as a proof of the innocence of its writer's relations with Murat in the past.   It certainly shows her amiably disposed toward Murat's wife at the time when it was written.

CHAPTER XIII

THE CONSULESSE

O^N the morning of February 19, 1800, Napoleon remarked to his secretary: " Well, Bourrienne, so to-day at last we are going to sleep in the Tuileries ! " He turned next to Josephine, gave her a playful pinch, as he delighted to do, and then threw his arms about her. No doubt the move was no surprise to either of his listeners. Everything since the 18 *brumaire* had pointed to the aggrandisement of the military member of the Consulate, the pike among the other fish.[1] Rather than play Second and Third Consuls to Napoleon's First, Sieyès and Ducos had resigned, and had been replaced by the more accommodating Cambacères and Lebrun. It was as First Consul by title, as well as in fact, that Napoleon transferred his

---

[1] In the early days of the new Government, Mme. Permon had observed to her old friend Letizia Bonaparte : " The pike will eat the other fish." All that Mme. Bonaparte could find to say in reply was : " Oh, Panoria ! "

NAPOLEON BONAPARTE, FIRST CONSUL.

From an engraving after Appiani.

p. 264.

residence from the Petit-Luxembourg to the
Tuileries. That home of the kings of France
had been renamed the Palais du Gouvernement,
to avoid offence; and not only Napoleon Bonaparte but also Lebrun was lodged there. But,
nevertheless, there was to be but one ruler
in the Palace now and for the next fourteen
years.

It was one o'clock on the day on which he
made the announcement to his secretary that
Napoleon left the Luxembourg, seated with Cambacères and Lebrun in a coach drawn by six
white horses, the gift of the Emperor to the
maker of the Treaty of Campo Formio. Josephine had been sent on ahead to the Tuileries,
and watched, from a seat to which Lebrun had
invited her in one of the windows of the
Pavilion of Flora, the arrival of the procession
in which she had no official position entitling
her to ride. Near her sat Hortense and two
other Beauharnais, Stephanie and Emilie, now
Mme. Lavalette; and, around, a number of
generals' wives and other prominent ladies, all
clad in the fashionable Greek costume of the day,
with light silk scarves over it. The Consuls'
coach drew up beneath their gaze, followed

by a long string of cabs with their numbers
obliterated and their origin disguised as well as
possible for the emergency; since Paris did
not possess carriages after the Revolution had
swept away such signs of aristocracy from
its midst. On arrival, the First Consul de-
scended from his coach and mounted a horse
which was waiting him. Then, with Murat and
Lannes at his side, he passed in review the
defiling regiments, saluting with bare head
the mutilated flags, while the crowd cheered
alike the troops and the Consul, and the
ladies waved their handkerchiefs from the
windows above. The review over, Napoleon
dismounted from his horse and entered the
Tuileries. That night, as they retired to rest,
Napoleon cried to Josephine : " Come along,
you little Creole, get into the bed of your
masters ! " So reports Mme. de Rémusat, the
recipient of so many confidences from her
Empress-patron in later years.

The " little Creole " slept in the bedroom of
Marie Antoinette on the ground floor of the
Tuileries, her other rooms adjoining it, while
Hortense had a small suite leading from her
mother's dressing-room.   Contrary to what had

been the case at the Luxembourg, at the Tuileries Napoleon had his rooms above his wife's, occupying the apartments which had belonged in turn to three Royal Louis. As at the Luxembourg, however, so at the Tuileries, Napoleon had a private staircase leading from his suite to Josephine's; here his study communicated with the stairs through a wardrobe which had once served Marie de Medici as an oratory. The First Consul intended to make no departure from his former domestic habits, and seldom made use of the large state bed reserved for him in the Royal apartments.

Where, however, their personal and intimate life was not concerned, the removal to the Tuileries was rapidly followed by great changes. Nothing showed this more clearly than the first reception of the foreign ambassadors two days after the move. Napoleon's valet, Constant, in his Memoirs thus describes the scene of February 21:

" At eight in the evening the apartments of Mme. Bonaparte were crowded with company. There was a dazzling display of splendid dresses, feathers, diamonds, etc. So great was the throng that it was found necessary to throw

open Mme. Bonaparte's bedchamber, the two
drawing-rooms being very small. When, after
considerable embarrassment and trouble, the
company had been arranged as well as possible,
Mme. Bonaparte was announced, and she
entered, conducted by M. de Talleyrand. She
wore a white muslin dress with short sleeves
and a pearl necklace, and her hair was braided
simply and confined by a tortoiseshell comb.
The murmur of admiration which greeted her
entrance must have been exceedingly gratifying
to her. I think she never looked more graceful
or elegant. M. de Talleyrand, still holding her
by the hand, presented her to the members of
the Diplomatic Body, one after another, not
introducing them by name, but designating them
by the courts which they represented. He
then led her round the two drawing-rooms.
They had not gone more than half round the
second room when the First Consul entered,
unannounced. He was dressed in a very plain
uniform coat, white cashmere breeches, and
top-boots. Round his waist he had a tricoloured
silk scarf with a fringe to match, and he carried
his hat in his hand. Amid the embroidered
coats, cordons, and jewels of the ambassadors

and foreign dignitaries, Bonaparte's costume appeared no less singular than did the simple elegance of Josephine's dress compared with the splendour of the ladies around her."

Josephine might well have contrasted now the position which she had held at the " court " of Barras and that which she now enjoyed as wife of the First Consul Bonaparte. Not all the changes were to her liking, no doubt. Napoleon continued to purge his wife's society of the characters who seemed to him undesirable. Jung, the editor of Lucien Bonaparte's Memoirs, represents Josephine as weeping to see herself reduced to the company of the wives of the great Government officials, " devoid of grace and very badly dressed " ; but Jung, like Lucien himself, is an unfriendly witness where Josephine is concerned. Society at the Tuileries was not limited to the dowdies. The Duchesse d'Abrantès mentions as prominent figures there at the time Mmes. de la Rochefoucauld, Lavalette, Lameth, Laplace, Luçay, Lauriston, d'Harville, Rémusat, and Talhouët. As for the young wives now for the first time intro- duced to society, we read of Josephine's kind reception of them all and her endeavours to

put them at their ease. If she had to mourn
the loss of agreeable friends like Mme. Tallien
and other stars of the Directory period, she had
at least compensation in her rank as the leading
woman in Paris. Still more important was her
position after her husband's brilliant success
in the Marengo campaign in the early summer
of 1800, on his return from which Mme. Permon
accused him of " playing the little king." He
still awaited the favourable moment for introducing a formal etiquette and for assigning to
his wife an official household. Nor did he
permit her to be more than a privileged spectator
at the commemoration of the fall of the Bastille
on July 14, eleven days after his return from
Italy. But in other respects she had ample
occasion for satisfaction with the progress of
her fortune.

Josephine's peace continued to be agitated
by the unending war with the Bonaparte family.
Truces might be declared from time to time,
as during the conspiracy of *brumaire*; but the
struggle was ever renewed after the reasons for
the truce had passed away. With Lucien in
particular the bitterest struggle endured. Lucien
Bonaparte had by his conduct on the 19 *brumaire*

LUCIEN BONAPARTE.
From a painting by R. Lefèvre at Versailles.

p. 270.

established a strong claim on the gratitude of
a brother who was never ungrateful to members
of his own family.   Yet within less than a year
from that date Lucien was deprived of the reward which his services had earned ; and in his
disgrace the hand of Josephine was not wanting.

Lucien had obtained the Ministry of the
Interior, an office for which his character fitted
him ill and in which he made many enemies.
His attachment to his personal friends, many
of whom qualified for the title by the patience
with which they listened to his poems and
romances, led him to reward them with posts
to which they had no claims whatever ; and
his unrestrained passion for opposition to the
established order of things, whatever it might
be, made him ready to listen to the suggestions
of his brother's ill-wishers and even put him
under suspicion of actual conspiracy against
the First Consul.   With Fouché, head of the
police, he was on the worst of terms.   Fouché
is one of the two men—Talleyrand is the other—
whose hold upon Napoleon, conscious of their
roguery, has never been satisfactorily explained.
But even without that hold now he had a strong
position in the contest with Napoleon's brother,

especially with the assistance which Josephine was ready to give him. She and Fouché were allies through common interests, and Fouché knew how to bind her firmly to him. It is alleged that the Minister of Police was already paying to her, as he undoubtedly seems to have paid later, a sum of a thousand francs a day in order that he might obtain from her information as to the secrets of the Tuileries. Fouché, as Napoleon's head spy, had no scruples against spying on his employer himself. Josephine was curiously destitute of scruples as to the manner in which she obtained money to meet the debts which she was afraid to acknowledge ; and we do not appear justified in rejecting the story of her acceptance of Fouché's bribes.

The downfall of Lucien was not accomplished with ease, in spite of his obvious abuse of his official position. His services had been great and he had a powerful ally in his mother, whose love for her third son was very strong. In the Petit-Luxembourg days Napoleon was disturbed by the opening movements of the struggle. Mme. Letizia came to him in great agitation one day, complaining that there was an organised campaign against Lucien. She

JOSEPH FOUCHÉ, DUC D'OTRANTO.
From a lithograph by Delpeche.

p. 272.

denounced Fouché as its originator. She did not venture to attack Josephine directly, but the latter, who was present when her mother-in-law called, was speedily reduced to tears. Before going the old lady turned to her and asked her to warn " her friend Fouché " that she, Mme. Bonaparte, thought her arms long enough to bring to repentance any one, whoever he might be, who slandered her sons.

Napoleon's absence in Italy delayed the crisis ; but it was not long in coming after his return. Josephine is said by some accounts to have taken upon herself to call her husband's attention to the harm which was being done to his government by the maladministration in the Ministry of the Interior, and to have persuaded him that it was necessary to take the portfolio away from his brother. She may have done so before Lucien himself rendered his position untenable. She had many opportunities denied to others of influencing Napoleon's mind, without definitely formulating a charge against her brother-in-law. Lucien is reported to have complained that his brother " put faith in the treacherous insinuations of a woman whom he ought to have known well enough not to sacrifice his family to her." But Lucien, apart from his official immorality or laxness, whichever one prefers to call it, made it impossible for himself to continue in his office for quite another reason.

It is now that we first begin to hear about the great question of Heredity, which was to be the cause of such bitter anguish to Josephine in the years to come. Already the First Consul had so established his position in the State that people wondered, and had commenced to discuss privately, to what end this one-man rule was tending. Was the Consulate of Napoleon to be prolonged? And if it were to be prolonged to the extent of his lifetime, who would be his successor? This was a matter in which friends and enemies alike were keenly interested ; and, naturally, none more so than his brothers and his wife. Josephine again found herself on the side of Fouché, who, like other ex-Jacobins, opposed a prolongation of office for Napoleon and the granting to him of the right to name his successor. It was not Republican sentiment which animated Josephine, however. She was no longer a *Sans-culotte Montagnarde*. She was only a wife who saw the danger of a divorce from a husband ruling France for life and allowed to choose his successor. Would he not desire to be succeeded by a son, and could she bear him such a son? If she could not, he had a remedy, which threatened ruin to her.

Napoleon's brothers, on the other hand, asked for nothing better than a life consulate for him and his right to name his successor. If he had no son to inherit from him, whom could he choose in preference to one of his own brothers? Lucien's gift of eloquence pointed him out as the spokesman of the family, and, confident in his own powers, he did not refuse the task of educating the public to the right point of view. The result was most unexpected by himself, and most gratifying to Josephine.

About the end of October 1800, the whole of official Paris was startled by the receipt from the Ministry of the Interior of an anonymous pamphlet entitled " A Parallel between Cæsar, Cromwell, and Bonaparte," in which the hereditary principle was warmly supported. Fouché arrived at the Tuileries with a copy and took it to the First Consul, proclaiming it a seditious

and dangerous publication. Napoleon sent for
his brother, between whom and Fouché there
was immediately a violent scene in his presence.
Angry at the attempt to force his hand, Napoleon, although he would not deny that the
pamphlet embodied some of his own ideas,
said that the man who had written the last
pages, in which the argument was most strongly
developed, was a fool. At this moment Josephine entered the room. Going over to Napoleon, she seated herself upon his knees and
passing her fingers through his hair said to
him : " I beg you, Bonaparte, not to make
yourself king. It is that dreadful Lucien
who is driving you to it. Don't listen to
him."

The combination of his official misconduct
and his premature monarchist activity was
too much for Lucien. He was removed from
the Interior, and, by way of a consolation, was
nominated to a special embassy to Madrid,
with a large salary attached to it. The final
scene before his departure is described by
Stanislas de Girardin, who was present at the
evening reception at the Tuileries on November 5, 1800—five days less than a year from

Lucien's great achievement at Saint-Cloud. In an armchair sat Josephine, looking thoughtful and striving to hide her satisfaction at what had come to pass. Opposite her was seated Hortense, frankly radiant with joy. Elisa Bacciochi, whose favourite brother was Lucien and who was to accompany her husband with Lucien to Madrid, was near at hand, with profound sorrow written on her face. She confided to Girardin that she was on the point of tears. He besought her to keep them back since they would so please " certain persons." The general air in the circle was one of constraint. The First Consul and the disgraced Minister had been in long conference in another room. They entered, Napoleon with a troubled face and disordered hair, Lucien showing an unnatural gaiety. In the sight of all present Lucien went up to his sister-in-law and spoke a few words in her ear. Then, before he left, he inquired of her what commissions she had for him in Madrid. She asked him for a few of the fans for which Spain was famous. As he went out, both she and Hortense were most gracious to him. She pressed Elisa's hand and embraced her. The scene was over.

Four days later, on the 18 *brumaire*, the embassy started for Madrid.

Lucien was out of the way, a victim partly to his own temerity. But the ideas which he had advocated remained. Napoleon, although he had consented to the disgrace of his brother, did not cease to devote attention to the question which excited so much interest in his own family and outside. However much he concealed the fact, he had for months been passing under review the possible candidates to succeed him when he should secure his supreme power for life. An outsider could scarcely be thought of, for to nominate such before his own death would be to raise up a rival in his lifetime. He might himself have a son. In default of issue, however, he must be prepared with some one else from his own family. Fond as he was of Joseph, he was quite aware of his very serious deficiencies. Lucien was plainly impossible. Louis was next, and it was greatly in his favour that, owing to his youth, he had not so far compromised himself in politics. Moreover, had not Louis's education been personally superintended by himself and appeared to him so successful that he had pronounced

him in 1791 to be " a man of forty, with all
the proper application and judgment " ? He
had not altered his opinion of the young man
nine years later. On the day after Lucien's
fall, Napoleon is reported to have said to an
intimate friend : " There is no further need to
rack our brains to find a successor. I have found
one—Louis. He has none of the faults of his
brothers, and he has all of their good qualities."

Events appeared to bring the question of
a successor to Napoleon increasingly to the
front. The First Consul had so many enemies
that it was not to be expected that all of them
would refrain from extreme measures in their
desire to get rid of him. A prematurely di-
vulged plot to assassinate him on his way
to the Opera in October 1800 was followed
by a very nearly successful effort in December,
which might have carried off Josephine as
well. It was Christmas Eve, and a performance
of Haydn's " Creation " was to take place at
the Opera. The Consular party rode in two
carriages from the Tuileries. In the first were
Napoleon, Bessières, Lannes, and young Lebrun,
son of the Third Consul. In the other were
Josephine, Hortense, Caroline Murat, and the

aide-de-camp Rapp. Josephine had lately received from Constantinople a new shawl, which
she was wearing that night. Rapp began to
explain to her how such shawls were worn in
Egypt, and before they left the Tuileries endeavoured to fasten hers for her in the fashion
he described. Owing to this delay at the
start Josephine's carriage was further behind
the other than it would otherwise have been.
This trivial circumstance perhaps saved her
life. As the First Consul entered the rue
Saint-Nicaise a cab and an old cart, coming
from the cross road, were on the point of block-
ing the way. One of the Consular escort
forced the cab out of the path of Napoleon's
carriage, which passed on rapidly. Immediately a loud explosion was heard. The cart
was loaded with a powder-barrel and had
blown up. The windows of the first carriage
were broken, but no other harm was done to
it. The second was close enough behind to
feel the shock, too ; its windows were shattered,
and Hortense received a slight cut on the
hand from the glass. Josephine fainted, but
she was unhurt. In the street eight people
were killed and twenty-eight wounded.

Napoleon took the affair very calmly. He hastened up the stairs, as usual, to show himself in the box before the arrival of the ladies. His only remark was : " These rascals wanted to blow me up. Fetch me a book of the oratorio." He had apparently been satisfied that the second carriage was safe and wished to prove immediately by his presence in the Opera House that the attempt had failed. Josephine arrived in tears and with signs of the shock plainly visible on her face, but sat through the performance at her husband's side.

The outrage of the rue Saint-Nicaise, although it had done no injury except to a few harmless passers-by, drew additional attention to the fact that Napoleon had no successor. He had not quite abandoned hope that he might have an heir by Josephine, though she was thirty-eight and the doctors were not encouraging. They advised another course of waters for the summer of 1801, and it was decided that she should go again to Plombières. But before this Josephine had begun to put into execution a plan by which she trusted that she might secure her position as wife of the First Consul, even if it should prove that she was incapable of bearing him a child.

Napoleon, as has been seen, had come to the conclusion that of all his family Louis was the one most suitable to be his heir, in default of direct issue. Some have attributed the suggestion to Josephine ; but there was no need to point out to Napoleon the merits of his brother. It is quite likely that Josephine welcomed the idea of making Louis the reversionary heir, and she certainly schemed to turn it to her own advantage. Louis was unmarried. Why should he not take Hortense to wife and so help to bind more closely the Bonaparte and Beauharnais families ? He had been supposed to feel rather bitterly the refusal of the hand of Emilie Beauharnais, and might be consoled by marriage with her cousin. Napoleon approved of the plan. It only remained to persuade Louis and Hortense.

Here, however, difficulties were encountered. Neither party showed an inclination to the match. Louis, after his early promise in France and Italy, had suffered a great change of character after an illness which befell him in 1797. His family, especially his brother Napoleon,

appeared to consider the change a passing
phase and his new attitude toward life a mere
pose. They refused to recognise that he had
become in reality a sentimental hypochondriac,
morose, jealous, and vain. Change of air
seemed to them the best cure. Louis agreed
to go on a year's tour in Germany and Northern
Europe, and started off in October 1800. It
is not known whether he had yet received any
hint of the marriage which his brother and his
sister-in-law had in view. His tour was un-
expectedly cut short. At the end of January,
a month after the attempt in the rue Saint-
Nicaise, he reappeared in Paris, saying that he
was ill. He took a country house, not far from
Paris, but away from the public roads and difficult of access through marsh and woodland.
Here he shut himself up until March. Then he
announced that he wished to join his regiment
in Portugal. An invitation to visit Malmaison
first could not be refused, and he spent a fort-
night there. At the end he left the château
in the middle of one night. His conduct was
mysterious, and the easiest explanation is that
he was troubled by the scheme for his future.
He was a young man who formed many senti-

mental attachments, and Constant (who, as
Napoleon's valet, could of course speak with
authority) claims that up to the very time
of his wedding he was interested in a girl
whom he had met casually in the Tuileries
gardens, the daughter of an inspector of
bridges.

The departure of Louis gave Josephine no
opportunity of completing her arrangement
for her daughter's marriage, and she left for
Plombières in the summer with all still in a
state of uncertainty. An amusing letter is preserved by Bourrienne which obviously belongs
to this period, although he attributes it to 1802,
an impossible date.[1] It is dated simply 21
messidor and is signed by Josephine Bonaparte,
Beauharnais-Lavalette (*i.e.* Emilie), Hortense
Beauharnais, Rapp, and Bonaparte *mère*. Addressed to "The Inhabitants of Malmaison,"
it runs as follows :

"The whole party left Malmaison in tears,
which brought on such dreadful headaches that
all the amiable persons were overcome by the

---

[1] Because in 1802 Hortense (then married to Louis) remained behind at Malmaison while Josephine went to Plombières.

thought of the journey. Mme. Bonaparte *mère* bore the fatigues of this memorable day with the greatest courage ; but Mme. Bonaparte, *consulesse*, exhibited none. The two young ladies who sat on the *dormeuse* were rival claimants to a bottle of eau-de-cologne ; and every now and then the amiable M. Rapp stopped the carriage for the comfort of his poor sick little heart, overflowing with bile ; finally he had to take to bed on arriving at Épernay, while the rest of the amiable party tried to drown their sorrows in champagne. The second day was more fortunate in the matter of health and spirits, but provisions were wanting and the sufferings of the stomach were great. The travellers lived on hopes of a good supper at Toul ; but their despair reached its height when on arrival they found only a miserable inn with nothing in it. We saw some odd-looking people there, which consoled us a little for spinach dressed in lamp-oil and red asparagus fried in curdled milk. Who would not have been amused to see the gourmands of Malmaison seated at a table so shockingly served ?

" Nowhere in history is there to be found the

record of a day of such dreadful distress as that on which we reached Plombières. On our departure from Toul we meant to breakfast at Nancy, for every stomach had been empty for two days ; but the civil and military authorities came to meet us and prevented the execution of our plan. We continued our journey, wasting away, so that you might see us growing thinner every minute. To complete our misfortune, the *dormeuse*, which seemed to have taken a fancy to embark on the Moselle for Metz, barely escaped overturning. But at Plombières we have been well recompensed for our unlucky journey, for on arrival we were welcomed with all kinds of rejoicings. The town was illuminated, the guns fired, and the faces of beautiful women at every window give us reason to hope that we shall support our absence from Malmaison with less regret.

"With the exception of some anecdotes, which we reserve for conversation on our return, you have here a correct account of our journey, to which we, the undersigned, hereby certify."

This frivolous account, which seems to be the composition of the two younger ladies, with

perhaps the collaboration of General Rapp, terminated with two postscripts :

" The company begs pardon for blots.

" It is requested that the person who receives this journal shall show it to all who take an interest in the fair travellers."

After her visit to Plombières with this lively set of companions, among whom one would imagine the grave Mme. Bonaparte *mère* rather misplaced, Josephine went to Vichy before returning to Paris to resume her matrimonial schemes on behalf of Hortense. Her own hopes, if she entertained any, of the beneficial effect of the course of waters were not gratified, and it was more than ever important that she should secure a new hold over Napoleon, even if it had to be secured at the price of amiability to one of those brothers who had since her marriage given her many proofs of their malevolence toward her.

CHAPTER XIV

JOSEPHINE AND HER CHILDREN

THE fact that Josephine arranged a marriage for her daughter with a man for whom she had no liking (having, indeed, met him very seldom), and with whom she subsequently found it impossible to live in harmony, has been taken as a confirmation of the accusation made by some of her contemporaries that she was not a good mother to her children—such contemporaries, for instance, as the Duchesse d'Abrantès, who writes : " I do not claim that she did not love Hortense. God preserve me from uttering such a thought ! Still, I have my memories, and these memories bring back to me words, facts, and things which I do not believe compatible with a mother's love such as Hortense should have inspired." Josephine, she continues, was the only one who did not seem to recognise the charm and attraction of her own daughter. The dislike which the Duchesse bore toward

QUEEN HORTENSE.

From an engraving after the picture by Girodet.

p. 288.

Josephine is apparent in these sentences. But
we must not on that ground entirely reject what
she says, especially as we find suggestions of a
somewhat similar kind, less unkindly put, in
other writers.

What, then, gave rise to the idea that Josephine was not a good mother ? We hear of no
definite act which can be described as unkind.
It is true that we find Hortense at certain periods
confided to the care of others ; for instance, to
that of the Princess of Hohenzollern-Sigmarin-
gen at Saint-Martin, Artois, in 1791, and, after
the death of Alexandre de Beauharnais, to that
of Mme. Campan. In 1791, however, Paris
was scarcely a safe spot for children ; and there
was nothing unusual in the despatch of Hortense
to a boarding-school in 1795, even if it were
more convenient for her mother to have no
child living with her during her intimacy with
Barras. Nor can it be said that any letters
from Josephine which have been published
give the slightest hint of unkindness. They
are all full of the fondest endearments—" my
child, my Hortense," " my good little Hortense,"
" my cherished daughter "—and of prayers for
speedy meeting. It is true that the letters to

her daughter were selected for publication by
that daughter herself. Nevertheless, the note
of tender affection sustained for so many years
is remarkable ; if it had become a habit, it
was a very agreeable habit.

As far as it is possible to judge, the real
meaning of the accusation against Josephine
is that she was unfitted by nature to guide her
children's lives. This is true, and the children
themselves recognised the fact in a praiseworthy manner. Both Eugène and Hortense
early grew accustomed to a reversal of the
maternal and filial relations. Josephine was
already to them, before they reached nominal
years of discretion, like a wayward charge for
whom their love must find excuses. They had
a firm belief in her affection for them, but they
knew that they were her protectors, not she
theirs. Eugène, even at the age of seventeen,
was full of the sense of responsibility which such
a position entailed. Can we not see this in the
already quoted letter of July 24 from Egypt,
and particularly in two of the sentences which
conclude that letter : " For six weeks no
news, no letters from you, from my sister, or
from any one. You must not forget us, mamma,

you must think of your children." Throughout his correspondence with her the same tone
prevails, always respectful, always loving, but
at the same time always admonitory. His
affectionate and loyal nature—strange issue
from the union of Alexandre de Beauharnais,
who was neither affectionate nor loyal, and
Josephine, in whose character loyalty was not
a strong feature, whatever view we take of her
affectionateness !—never let Eugène cease from
advising, supporting, and defending the spoilt
creature whom fate had given him as a mother.
She grew to rely on him in a way in which she
relied on no one else, and at the end of her career
as Empress it was not until she had seen Eugène
and heard him discuss the question with Napoleon
that she recognised what he had long seen, that
she must bow to the inevitable and accept the
divorce with what calm she could assume.

The relative positions of mother and children
were impressed upon them very strongly after
Napoleon's return from Egypt. Eugène well
aware, Hortense probably unaware, of the
charges against their mother, they had jointly
saved her from a shameful fate. Frequently
afterwards it fell to the lot of Hortense (who,

unlike Eugène, was so much at her mother's side) to shield Josephine against Napoleon in less serious situations than that at the rue de la Victore in October 1799. Napoleon made no protest against this attitude of his step-daughter, but even welcomed it. He had a perfectly genuine paternal feeling for her, which she for many years scarcely understood and his enemies most basely misrepresented. Mme. de Rémusat, however, does it justice when she writes : " He who seldom had a high opinion of women always professed respect for Hortense, and the way in which he spoke of her and acted toward her gives the lie very explicitly to the accusations made against her. In her presence his language was always more guarded and proper. He often called her in as judge between his wife and himself, and accepted from her lessons which he would have taken from no one else patiently. ' Hortense,' he sometimes said, ' compels me to believe in virtue.' "

Napoleon's estimate of his step-daughter was doubtless too high, just as that of some of her other relatives by marriage was too low. Lucien Bonaparte writes of her that at the time of her wedding she was " very advanced for her age in knowledge of the world (*les choses d'ici-bas*)," and, as we shall see, did not hesitate to make a disgraceful imputation against her, which her unhappy husband afterwards could not banish from his mind. What she would have become with a reasonable man in the place of Louis it is difficult to say. Gifted with a sweet and loving disposition, she was easily affected by cold treatment, and still more by such injustice and jealousy as she received from Louis. Her ultimate lapse from the strait path of morality, of which the result was the illegitimate half-brother of Napoleon III. known to history as the Duc de Morny, was, if not excusable, at least intelligible in one of her disposition.

In appearance Hortense is described as pleasing rather than beautiful. She had too large a nose, a poorly shaped mouth, and, like her mother, bad teeth. On the other hand, she had a slight, elegant figure, fair hair of great beauty, and large eyes of violet-blue. Two years before her marriage the Duchesse d'Abrantès writes of her as "really charming at this time of her life" and as uniting the graces of the Creole and the French woman. She had imbibed whatever there was of education to be obtained at the academy of Saint-Germain-en-Laye, where she was a pupil dear to Mme. Campan's heart. She danced, drew, painted, and sang with equal facility, could play both piano and harp, and, as she showed later, could compose music ; " Partant pour la Syrie " survives as an example of her skill. Nor were her literary pretensions altogether contemptible. With more strength of character (which could hardly be expected of a daughter of Alexandre de Beauharnais and Josephine) she might have made for herself in reality the honoured name which her Imperial son piously claimed for her after her death. More strength of character, too, might have led her to resist the *mariage de convenance* to which she was persuaded by her mother, her step-father, and others who called themselves her friends.[1] But nature furnished her with

---

[1] Mme. Campan, for instance, counselled her to strict obedience to the wishes of Napoleon. " I beg you to see," wrote the preceptress to her pupil of former days, "that in everything your conduct and Eugène's may satisfy the First Consul as regards his views for the settlement of you two. You are one of the dearest bonds between him and your mamma, and should you fall into disgrace and negligence, do not think that you will ever find consolation. One may dispense with reaching a high position, nay, one may even feel that it is a happiness to live remote from such ; but one cannot come down again with sorrow. This is a great truth."

no power of resistance against those who treated her kindly.

The autumn of 1801 saw the consummation of Josephine's desire to marry Hortense to Louis Bonaparte. Lucien claims [1] that she first made an attempt to secure him for her daughter. His bitter hatred for Josephine makes his story suspicious, especially as we know that Josephine was aware of a proposal from Lucien to Napoleon to find him another wife in her place. He says, however, that, soon after his return from Spain (he came back in November 1801, having accumulated fifty million francs, it was reported), he was invited to breakfast by Josephine. She was very gracious to him, and, in the presence of the blushing Hortense, openly hinted at a match. Lucien was guarded in his replies and let her know that he did not contemplate a second marriage after his loss of Christine. Josephine did not insist, but the arrival of the First Consul put an end to an embarrassing situation.

Unfortunately for Lucien's reputation for truth, it seems probable that Hortense was

[1] "Mémoires," ii. 268.

already engaged to Louis when his elder brother
returned from Madrid. Louis was back in
Paris in September, and at a dance at Malmaison yielded to the wishes of Napoleon and
Josephine and asked Hortense to be his wife.
He claims in his Memoirs to have been forced
into an engagement. But he is scarcely more
trustworthy than Lucien; and what he says
in his Memoirs, moreover, is coloured by his
subsequent quarrels with his wife. At the
time of the engagement, whatever may have
been his state of mind before and after, he
was generally supposed to have fallen in love
with Hortense. Even Lucien bears witness
to this.[1] With his peculiar delicacy of feeling
he ventured to suggest to Louis that there
might be reasons for the anxiety of Hortense's
mother and step-father to marry her; but
Louis could only stammer that he was already
in love. " You are in love ? " Lucien says
that he replied. " Then why the devil do you
come to ask my advice ? Forget what I have
told you. Marry her and God bless you ! "

The insinuation which Lucien had not scrupled
to make was one of singular infamy; but, as

[1] "Mémoires," ii. 269.

it remained in the unhappy mind of Louis and helped to poison him against his wife, it must be explained here. Lucien repeated the story which some of the vilest scandal-mongers had invented against Napoleon—that he was himself in love with Hortense.[1] Louis took no notice of this very base falsehood at the time, and it was not until he discovered their incompatibility of character that it recurred to him. Then he was morbidly inclined to receive every suspicion.

Bourrienne, no more truthful but less actuated by malice in distorting facts than the Bonaparte brothers, has yet another account of the way in which the engagement between Louis and Hortense was brought about. Hortense, he says, was smitten with Duroc, one of Napoleon's aides-de-camp ; and he himself acted as their intermediary in carrying letters unknown to Napoleon or Josephine. Hortense's desire, how-

---

[1] And indeed that he was the father of her first child. M. Masson easily disproves this by an exposition of dates (" Napoléon et les Femmes," 178). Lucien, it may be noted, after describing his interview with Louis, says : " Eight days later Louis was married. It was a case of urgency." But for the existence of his own Memoirs it might be possible to feel some sympathy with Lucien ; but they leave him with hardly a rag of decent character.

ever, was not secret, and at length on January 4,
1802, Napoleon consented to let her marry the
man of her choice, if Duroc wished it ; if not,
she must marry Louis. Duroc, when he was
told that it was an essential condition that he
must go to live at Toulon—" I don't want a
son-in-law in my house," said Napoleon—
refused. The same night before they went
to bed Napoleon told Josephine that Hortense
must wed Louis, which was what Josephine
herself wanted.

That Hortense had an attachment for Duroc
is true, but the rest of Bourrienne's tale [1] seems
drawn largely from his imagination. Hortense
only admits that Duroc wished to marry her,
that she was not unwilling, and that Murat
(not Bourrienne) conveyed a letter from him
to her before he went away on a mission for
Napoleon to Berlin. Hortense was afraid to
open the letter and left it in her room. On
going downstairs in the evening, she was greeted
by the First Consul with the remark : " These
are nice things I hear. You receive love-letters
without your parents' consent ! " She burst

[1] It is very much compressed above. See Bourrienne, iv.
319–21.

into tears. After teasing her for a little, Napoleon relented. It was agreed to send Duroc's letter back to him unread, and the affair ended.

There are thus numerous contradictory versions of the manner in which Josephine's scheme was brought to a successful issue. But she gained her end. " My daughter can only marry a prince or a Bonaparte," she is said to have remarked. On January 3, 1802, the marriage contract was drawn up, and on the following day Hortense became the wife of Louis Bonaparte.[1] Little more than three years later she was a princess.

---

[1] " Never was a ceremony more gloomy," says Louis in his Memoirs. " Never did husband and wife feel such misgivings about a forced and ill-assorted match." But these words were written long after the marriage had come to a disastrous end.

CHAPTER XV

UNWELCOME HONOURS

THE wedding of Louis Bonaparte and
Hortense Beauharnais was marked by
a religious ceremony in addition to the civil
contract ; and at the same time the marriage
of Caroline with Murat, which had up to the
present been purely civil, was now, by Napoleon's order, blessed by the Church. Napoleon
did not, however, suggest that a similar course
should be adopted with regard to his own
union with Josephine. It may be imagined
that the significance of this was not lost upon
Josephine, little though she may have been
troubled by religious scruples, which hardly
were a part of her nature. The growing respect
paid by Napoleon for religious forms, which
was to be strikingly illustrated soon, can but
have made this neglect to ratify his own marriage in the eyes of Christians painfully suspicious to his wife. She knew, moreover,

LOUIS BONAPARTE, KING OF HOLLAND.
From a lithograph after Bellard.

p. 300

that Lucien while at Madrid had proposed to his brother a marriage with the Infanta Isabella of Spain. Napoleon had rejected the proposal, not without mentioning it to Josephine. But what warrant had she that another suggestion might not prove more tempting to him, since, if he were not open to such suggestions, why should he not give to his union with her that sanction which he considered necessary in the cases of his brother Louis and his sister Caroline? It must have been with a troubled heart that Josephine saw her husband start on January 8, four days after Louis's wedding, to meet the envoys of the Cisalpine Republic at Lyon, and to receive from them the offer of their Presidency. Every step upward for Napoleon brought an added dread to his childless wife. Even when they first moved to the Tuileries, she is reported to have trembled and exclaimed that "to climb so high was to expose oneself to giddiness"; and now it was plain that the climbing must continue, whither she could not see.

Still, in spite of the terror of divorce which must always have been at her heart, she had no reason to complain that Napoleon did not

make her state increase with his own. When
the move was made from the Petit-Luxembourg
to the Tuileries, Josephine had no official
position at all, and, although she was hostess
at a virtual Court, had no Household over
which to preside. At the Tuileries a gradual
development of her position began, which
was manifested also at Malmaison, where in
May 1801 she entertained with Napoleon the
newly created King of Etruria and his wife.
A Bourbon at last was the guest of the Josephine who had failed as the Vicomtesse de
Beauharnais to be admitted to the Bourbon
Court at Paris. In the chief festivals of the
year—the fête of the Republic on July 14, and
the commemoration of *brumaire* on November 9
—she had the most prominent place among
the women. But it was not until after Napoleon's return from Lyon in February 1802 that
he decided to brave public opinion and establish
a regular Court etiquette and a Household
in the Palace. Josephine now had assigned
to her four " Ladies of the Palace," each of
whom attended on her for a week at a time,
while all four were present on great occasions,
such as when the ambassadors' wives and

other distinguished visitors were to be presented to her. All her ladies had aristocratic names which must have been dear to her— Lauriston, Luçay, Rémusat, Talhouët—and which at the same time were calculated to impress those who were inclined to look askance at a Republican First Consul's wife. Scoffers were more silent when they saw at her receptions an etiquette modelled on the presentations to the Queens of France, a host of green-and-gold liveried servants, and a regular palace staff of Governor and prefects, all generals, of aides-de-camp, and of ladies of old family.

Nowhere was the change in Josephine's condition more conspicuous than at the great ceremony of Easter 1802, when Napoleon signalised his reconciliation with religion by a solemn *Te Deum* at Notre-Dame. In the previous year, Joseph Bonaparte and Cardinal Consalvi had drawn up the terms of the Concordat, which was promulgated in April after its acceptance by the State bodies. On the day of the service an audience was given to the Cardinal Legate, who after visiting the First Consul was received also by his wife.

It was observed that Josephine did not advance
to meet the Legate, but merely rose from her
chair twice, as he came in and went out. All
the details had been arranged beforehand by
Napoleon. Time was not yet ripe for Josephine
to ride with him in the procession ; but, accompanied by more than sixty ladies of the
highest positions in France, she proceeded to
the place reserved for her in the gallery of the
church. So brilliant was the scene there that
Napoleon remarked at the Tuileries that he
recommended to painters the picture of the
gallery of Notre-Dame on April 18, 1802. In
the centre of all Josephine should have sat,
but on her arrival she found that Mme. Hulot,
mother-in-law of Moreau, the hero of Hohen-
linden, had taken her place and refused to
move. Josephine, who desired to conciliate the
old lady, took another seat ; but Napoleon,
when he observed what he described as " the
nut-cracker face and evil expression " of Mme.
Hulot where his wife should have been, exhibited signs of bad temper which continued
to the end of the service.

The procession which went to Notre-Dame
was the most gorgeous since the Revolution,

if it were not to be compared to that which
went from the Tuileries to the same place some
two years and a half later. For the first time
since the old *régime* had disappeared liveries
were seen in the streets, the green of Napoleon's
household, the red and blue of the other Consuls,
the yellow of the various great officials, etc.
Four-horse carriages drew the Councillors of
State, Ambassadors, and Ministers, six horses
the Second and Third Consuls, and eight horses
Napoleon himself, clad in scarlet velvet coat
and black breeches, with a tricolour plume in
his hat. Inside the church four battalions of
troops waited, and the *Te Deum* was accompanied by drums and trumpets within and the
firing of artillery without. It was long before
the service, which Napoleon had ordered to be
conducted with the fullest possible pomp,[1]
came to an end. After all, the Bonaparte

[1] Too much for many of those present, it would appear.
Bourrienne remarks on the irreverence of part of the con-
gregation, the whisperings and even open murmurs during the
ceremony. It was not so easy for others as for Napoleon to
break away from the anti-religious habits of the Revolution.
But the others did not comprehend like Napoleon the importance of winning over from the Bourbon cause the clergy—
" one of our best weapons," as the Bourbon claimant wrote to
the Comte d'Artois.

family, husbands and wives, drove to Mortefontaine to dine with Joseph, the nominal
concluder of the Concordat.

In the midst of all the splendour and move-
ment of the time we get continual glimpses of
the undying strife between Bonaparte and
Beauharnais, that Fourteen Years' War which
raged about the person of Napoleon and was
only suspended when the belligerents were
temporarily distracted by their own interests
to some other occupation. The question of
turning the First Consulship into a life office,
which was more and more discussed as time
went on, furnished a grand occasion for a new
outbreak of hostilities between Josephine and
the Bonaparte brothers. The defeat of Lucien,
which had resulted in his financially profitable
exile to Spain, was not accepted by him or the
others as final. Circumstances fought on their
side, and as they saw success approaching,
they grew triumphant in anticipation. Bourrienne describes their pretensions as incredible
and relates how one day Lucien, asked by
Josephine why he had not come to dinner at
the Tuileries on the previous evening, answered :
" Because there was no seat reserved for me.

The brothers of Napoleon ought to have the first place after him."

Mme. de Rémusat tells another tale of disputed precedence at a dinner given by Joseph Bonaparte at Mortefontaine about this period. On this occasion Napoleon appears as one of the combatants in the warfare. The family was assembled, including Mme. Letizia, and when dinner was announced Joseph offered his arm to his mother, asking Lucien to take in Josephine. Napoleon at once remarked that Joseph must put his mother on his left hand and his sister-in-law on his right. The elder brother took no notice, and the party was going into the dining-room as he had arranged, when Napoleon crossed over rapidly to Josephine, took her from Lucien, and walking in with her first, sat down to table with her at his side. A coldness fell upon the guests, but Napoleon called to Mme. de Rémusat, who was in attendance on Josephine, and asked her to sit on his other side. As she was a stranger this at least avoided any further dispute. But it is not surprising to hear that cordial feeling was absent from the dinner-table and that Josephine confessed to her lady that she was glad when it came to an end.

Petty victories, sought or unsought for by herself, over the pretensions of the Bonapartes could not console Josephine for the inevitable approach of an event which she dreaded. After the Senate had voted a further term of ten years, which by no means satisfied Napoleon, the Council of State decided in May that it was time to ask France to settle by plebiscite the question whether the First Consul should hold his office for life. Josephine confided her anxieties to all who would listen to her. " Bonaparte's real enemies," she told Roederer, " are those who put into his head ideas about a dynasty, about heredity, divorce, and a second marriage." " Bonaparte listens to me with sufficient attention," she said on another occasion to one of the Councillors of State, " but his flatterers soon alter his opinions for him. The generals exclaim that they have not fought against the Bourbons merely to substitute the Bonapartes for them. I do not at all regret that I have given my husband no children, since I should tremble for their fate. I shall remain attached to the destiny of the Bona-

partes," she continued, "however perilous it
be, as long as he cherishes for me the regard
and friendship which he has always shown.
But the day on which he changes I shall leave
the Tuileries."

Fouché was also the recipient of her confidences ; but, however much he agreed with
her in opposing the idea of a life Consulship,
he saw that all efforts to thwart Napoleon
would be in vain. Since the course of events
could not be stopped, let it go on. He had
no other advice to give. As enemies of the
scheme on foot, both he and she were for the
time out of the inner ring. He probably fore-
saw his own coming fall from the Ministry and
that Josephine could not help him. She had
defended him at the time of the rue Saint-
Nicaise outrage, when he had been accused of
neglecting his duty. But now she was hardly
in a position even to earn the daily pension
which he allowed her to keep him informed
of what went on at the Tuileries or at Malmaison. Napoleon was putting her on false
scents, it was said, in order that she might
mislead his Minister of Police—a truly remarkable position of affairs ! Whether or not

it was true (as M. Masson, for instance, maintains) that her sensual influence over him was waning, he certainly avoided for the moment the risk which was threatened by trusting his thoughts to her. In a corresponding degree Lucien was readmitted to his confidence, whence he had been banished since his misbehaviour as Minister of the Interior. It was useless for Josephine to complain. " How can you trust Lucien ? " she asked. " Have you not told me yourself that you saw a letter written by him to his uncle, in which he threatened your life ? Have you not told me that Lucien would be nothing as long as you were First Consul ? " " Attend to your spinning ! " was Napoleon's only reply.

There was nothing for Josephine to do in Paris. She could not check the course of events, as Fouché had told her, and she might as well go away as stay where she was not for the moment wanted. There were always the waters. Corvisart, the doctor, would not pronounce it impossible for Plombières to aid in a matter which caused her so much sorrow, whatever she might say with ulterior motives to Councillors of State. While she remained in

the family circle, all keenly interested in the
discussion of subjects which filled her with
dread, there was little chance of her forgetting
that she was thirty-nine and that she had not
borne Napoleon a child. One day the question
of barrenness came up among the ladies. " You
forget," said Josephine, " that I have already
had children. Are not Eugène and Hortense
my children ? " " But you were young then,
my sister," replied Elisa Bacciochi. Josephine
had recourse to her never-failing remedy of
tears. In the middle Napoleon entered the
room and insisted on being told what was the
matter. " How indiscreet of you ! " he said
angrily to Elisa. " Do you not know that the
truth is not always good to tell ? "

Such intervention on the part of her husband
was worse than the original malice of her sister-
in-law ; and Josephine must have felt em-
barrassed, although the society in which she
had mixed had few reticences, at the public
discussion of her bodily state. For Napoleon
continued to talk in a most open way, in company including Lucien and several generals,
about the possibility of a child being born. It
was unlikely at her age, he told her jokingly,

even if he were not the father. Thereupon
Lucien joined in the conversation and remarked : " Now, my sister, show the Consul
that he is mistaken and give us quickly a little
Cæsarion ! " [1]

From such unwelcome conversations at least
Josephine escaped when she went to Plombières
about the middle of June. She left behind her
at Malmaison Hortense, in order that there
might be a hostess in charge. There survives
a letter from Napoleon to her at this epoch,
which is curiously worded and shows him in a
very tender mood, in spite of the alleged waning
of her dominion over him.

" I have not received any news from you,"
he writes, " but I suppose you must already
have begun to take the waters. We are a
little melancholy here, although your amiable
daughter does the honours of the house marvellously well. I have been for two days slightly
troubled with my pain. Your big Eugène ar-

---

[1] The account which Bourrienne says he had from Josephine
of this scene makes Lucien's suggestion to have been that
either she or Napoleon should have a child by some one else.
" The amiable Josephine," adds Bourrienne, " was sobbing as
she described the scene to me." In this case it seems better to
trust to Lucien's version, which is that given above. It
sounds more probable.

rived here yesterday. He is marvellously well.

" I love you as on the first day, because you are good and amiable above all things.

" Hortense tells me that she has written to you often.

" A thousand amiable messages and a kiss of love. Ever yours.

"BONAPARTE."

Before the end of July Josephine returned from Plombières to find that the plebiscite had already been taken which made Napoleon First Consul for the term of his life, although the result had not yet been made public. As she must have been expecting this, she had no doubt by now grown accustomed to the idea. She asked him when he was going to make her Empress of the Gauls, and he laughingly re-assured her as to her position. Whatever he had now in his head, he was not yet prepared to take her into his confidence. On August 4 the figures of the plebiscite were declared, showing that an overwhelming majority of his fellow-countrymen desired Napoleon to be Life Consul over them. At the Tuileries all was

rejoicing. The Bonaparte family was assembled there, and thither came visitors in
crowds to offer their congratulations. It was
observed that on Josephine's face more appre-
hension than joy was visible. Napoleonist
writers have commented unfavourably on this,
some quoting Bourrienne's criticism that "she
saw in each step which the First Consul made
toward the throne a step which took him farther
from her" as though it were a mark of her
selfish regard for her own interests alone. This
hardly seems just to Josephine. Although she
might have been better advised to mask her
thoughts, it was not unreasonable that she
should feel apprehensive as to what was in
store for her, with nothing except her husband's
love (and that possibly not so ardent of late)
standing between her and the divorce to which
many of his advisers, of his own kindred especially, were constantly urging him, in the
interests alike of State and of family.

Another point should be taken into consideration in connection with Josephine's du-
bious reception of the elevation of Napoleon
to the Life Consulship, which was already
Empire under a Republican name. It cannot

be supposed that her attachment to the Royalist cause was sufficiently strong to make her willing to sacrifice anything to it. Still, in spite of her erstwhile declarations of *sans-culotterie*, she had a genuine respect for the old *régime*. The ex-nobles had always found a friend in the widow Beauharnais, and they had continued to find one in Mme. Bonaparte. Such of the old aristocracy as could safely live in Paris were welcomed in her *salons*. Whether at the rue de la Victoire, the Petit-Luxembourg, or the Tuileries, it was the same. Those still expressing opinions favourable to the Bourbons knew that they would not be rejected by the First Consul's wife on that account. They knew she liked their manners and sympathised with their loyalty to the exiled family. They felt no compunction, therefore, in paying visits to her, even when they scornfully refused all dealings with the Consul himself. They re-ferred to her any petitions which they had to make, and she on her part delighted to forward them. It was always a pleasure to her to be a patroness, and particularly to an aristocratic client.

Nor did Josephine stop here. She even

allowed herself to be approached by Royalist
agents who hoped to be able to persuade General
Bonaparte, as they called him, to play the
Monk in a Bourbon restoration.   An interesting
letter has been published written in March 1801
by the Comte de Provence to one of his supporters, the Marquis de Clermont-Gallerande.
No one, the Comte wrote, could better persuade
General Bonaparte to re-establish the legitimate
monarchy than she whose lot was bound up
with his, who could only be happy at his happiness and honoured by his glory. " I did not
learn what is her way of thinking to-day. The
Comte de Vioménil, about whose sentiments
there can certainly be no doubt, has told me
more than once that at Martinique he often
urged her that her Royalism went beyond
prudence, and the assistance which she gives
to-day to those of my faithful subjects who
have recourse to her earns for her thoroughly
the name of angel of kindness which you give
to her. So make known to Mme. Bonaparte
my sentiments. They should not surprise her.
Either I am deceived or her heart will rejoice
at them."

.If the Comte de Provence could write thus

early in 1801, in 1802 Josephine was still more
eager to further the Bourbon restoration. Her
dream was to see Napoleon Constable of France
and herself a leading figure at a Legitimist
Court. Her rooms in the Tuileries were therefore always open in the mornings—for they
would not come in the evenings to mix with
the supporters of the Government—to adherents
and secret agents of the late Royal family.
In the spring of 1802 Napoleon discovered
something of this and ordered two ladies,
Mmes. de Damas and de Champcenetz, to be
put across the frontier. He welcomed Josephine's friendship with the old nobility, but
he had no mind to become a Constable of
France under the Bourbons ; moreover, there
was danger in the Royalist conspiracies, as
was to be seen before long.

In view of her fears and her ambitions alike,
we must not judge Josephine too harshly if she
could not enter joyfully into the celebrations
of August 1802, and if it was with somewhat
of terror that she saw the " star " of Napoleon
shining forty feet above Notre-Dame during
the illumination of the cathedral in honour of
his new dignity.

CHAPTER XVI

AN ANXIOUS PERIOD

IN the October following Napoleon's attainment of the Life Consulship, an event took place in the Bonaparte family which brought about a temporary improvement of relations between some of the warring members. On the 18 *vendémiare an XI.* (October 10, 1802) a child was born to Hortense and Louis Bonaparte, who was baptized Napoleon-Charles. Two hundred and eighty days had elapsed since the marriage of Hortense and Louis, and Josephine must have felt a great relief at the dispelling of the suspicions which Lucien and others had endeavoured to create concerning the " urgency " of that marriage. Napoleon had been keenly alive to the way in which he and his step-daughter had been slandered, since there was an attempt to revive the scandal while Hortense was doing the honours of Malmaison during her mother's absence at Plombières. It was perhaps in consequence of this that he decided that the birth of the child should not occur at the Tuileries or Malmaison, and took for her a new house in the rue de la Victoire rather larger than that which had been first Josephine's, next his, and lastly lent by him to his brother and Hortense. Accordingly it was in this house that Napoleon-Charles was born. The "Moniteur," for the first time in the history of the Bonaparte family, announced the occurrence with the mother's name printed in small capitals.

Josephine, it has been said, must have felt a great relief at the birth of her grandchild in due season. For it is impossible that she could be ignorant of the evil falsehood which it pleased some of the Bonapartes and the more unscrupulous Royalist enemies of the First Consul to spread about him and Hortense. It has been argued from the fact that Josephine later repeated the stories in moments of extreme agitation, that she was inclined to believe them. This appears an unwarranted deduction. What Josephine said when she was distracted by grief and what she believed in her sane condition were totally different things. She was a woman with singularly little power of repression when afflicted with sorrow or under the influence of a personal grievance ; and the troubles of the years preceding her divorce were calculated to disturb an equilibrium more constant than hers.

Louis Bonaparte came back to Paris three days before the birth of his son. He had begun to act in a strange manner very soon after his marriage. The early days with Hortense at 6 rue de la Victoire had been unpleasant for both of them. He lost no time before making a systematic attempt to detach Hortense from her mother's side. Granted that Louis shared the hatred of Joseph and Lucien for Josephine and that he despised her for her past levity of conduct, he acted very unwisely in show-ing his sentiments to a daughter who had so strong an affection for her mother as Hortense had for Josephine. He went still further, it is said, and told Hortense what he knew about Josephine's character. The effect was not what he apparently expected. She did not agree with Louis that she must break off relations with her mother. On the other hand, she now had no one to go to in her wretch-edness. Her dull-eyed, morose, imaginary in-valid of a husband had succeeded in cutting her off from the full sympathy of her former natural protectors, but he did not thereby draw her to himself. She could only nurse her grief in her own heart and find what consolation she might in society and her personal tastes. When Louis left her in the March after their wedding, upon the useful pretext of joining his regiment again, she could not bear the associations of their home, and was glad therefore to spend most of her time at the Tuileries and Malmaison until the advent of her first-born brought a distraction.

Napoleon-Charles's birth was followed by an improvement in his parents' domestic affairs. Louis could have no real doubt that the child was his, and for a little while he showed a distinctly tenderer feeling toward his wife. Even Josephine, who can hardly have been totally ignorant of Louis's intentions against herself, was satisfied by his improved attitude toward his wife, and for the present there was a harmony in the inner circle of the Bonaparte-Beauharnais family which was indeed rare.

There was, however, coming to be a new factor in the lives of Josephine and Napoleon which was destined to cause her much pain and

him much annoyance.   Josephine was growing
jealous.   The day had passed when his heart
was torn by her levity and actual unfaithfulness.
She had mended her ways, and she was in her
fortieth year.   He, on the other hand, was
little over thirty-three and the supreme ruler
of France, with temptations thrown daily in
his way.   He had shown no lessening of his
affectionate regard for her ; but his passion had
hardly survived the return from Egypt, had
even ceased to be exclusively hers before his
return.   If she could not retain her empire over
his senses, could she count upon his affection
to put aside the thought of a younger wife whom
so many counselled him to take, in the interests
of himself, his family, and the State ?   She
began to watch with an anxious eye for every
trace of infidelity to her, regardless of the fact
that whenever she made a scene the annoyance
drove Napoleon farther in the direction in which
she feared to see him go.   She failed for some
time (it is hardly unnatural) to appreciate his
reasoning that " she took things far too seriously
and ought not to make herself miserable about
amusements in which his affection had no part."

Mme. de Rémusat relates one of the scenes

which occurred at the Tuileries some time in
1803. Josephine suspected that one of the
actresses at the Théâtre-Français, Mlle. Georges,
had an attraction for her husband. Now it had
grown to be Napoleon's custom to go to bed
first and to send for Josephine, often as early as
11 o'clock. One night Josephine was waiting
in her own sitting-room with Mme. de Rémusat.
Midnight passed, and no summons came from
Napoleon. Josephine grew more and more
agitated. At last she turned to her lady and
said : " I can bear it no longer. Mlle. Georges
is there. I want to surprise them. Follow
me ; we will go up together." Mme. de Rémusat's protests were unavailing, and Josephine
dragged her along with her to the secret staircase and up the stairs. All was in darkness, but
suddenly a slight noise was heard. " Perhaps it
is Bonaparte's mameluke Rustan, guarding
his door," whispered Josephine fearfully. " The
wretch is capable of killing us both." Mme.
de Rémusat yielded to panic and this time
dragged her mistress with her down the stairs.
When they were back in the sitting-room
Josephine abandoned the idea of a surprise.
Napoleon, however, came to hear of the affair

and insisted that in future he and she must occupy their own separate rooms. Josephine, in her grief, urged that she was afraid for his safety, and that as she was a light sleeper it was to his advantage to have her with him. But he would not give way.

Mme. de Rémusat, who has preserved this anecdote, was herself for a short period suspected by Josephine of attracting the regard of Napoleon. He undoubtedly took pleasure in the conversation of the good-looking lady of honour, who was only twenty-two when she entered Josephine's service in 1802, and saw much of her society during a month in camp at Boulogne, whither she had come to nurse her husband, lying ill there. Josephine was decidedly cold to her on her return ; but she had no reason for fear, since Mme. de Rémusat was a warm adherent of the wife against the husband, and her Memoirs are strongly coloured by the innumerable confidences which Josephine made to her during their long association.[1] She had

---

[1] Mme. de Rémusat burnt her original Memoirs during the Hundred Days, fearing, it was said, that the anti-Napoleonist tone, which her indignation at the divorce of Josephine had inspired, might be the cause of trouble to her. She wrote the Memoirs which now survive in 1818.

met Josephine at Croissy, where her mother,
Mme. Gravier de Vergennes, widowed by the
Terror, had a house ; and, in spite of the
disparity in age, the two became warm friends.
The incident at Boulogne only caused a slight
estrangement between them. " Clari "—her
real name was Claire-Elisabeth-Jeanne—was too
sympathetic a recipient of her complaints for
Josephine to lose her over a misunderstanding
for which she was in no way responsible. To
no one else was she so ready to impart
her ever-increasing suspicions against her
husband.

It was but natural that there should be found
people ready, out of friendship or malice, to
inform Josephine that Napoleon had cast his
eyes in this or that direction. And hence-
forward, by a strange reversal, the man who had
written to his wife in 1796 to " beware the
dagger of Othello," was doomed to be harassed
by the tongue of a jealous woman. Lucien has
in his Memoirs a story which may be true,
although there is one unexpected feature in it.
He says that Napoleon one day had been im-
portuned by Josephine's complaints and remarked to her : " Imitate Livia and you will

find me an Augustus." "What does he mean about Livia ? " asked the weeping Josephine of Joseph and Lucien—surely curious consolers for her to seek ! "Imitate Livia," was their only reply ; and Lucien adds : "It is said that she followed our advice. It was the best thing she could do."

However, the best distraction from the torments of jealousy for Josephine was undoubtedly that Napoleon should be occupied in public affairs which would leave him little time for love. This was not long in coming.   On April 14, 1803, a diplomatic reception was to be held at the Tuileries.   Josephine was in her private apartments, completing her toilet, with Mme. de Rémusat in attendance.   The First Consul, present as so often while his wife dressed in the evening, was sitting on the floor playing with the six-months-old baby Napoleon-Charles.   A message came that the guests were waiting. "Come, ladies ! " said Napoleon, with an abrupt change of manner ; and with a pale and contracted face he walked hastily into the *salon*. He made straight for Lord Whitworth, the English Ambassador, and in the midst of the great official gathering cried to him : "So you

are decided upon war! We have had it for
ten years, you want it for another ten, and you
are forcing me to it." Josephine and her
attendant lady exchanged glances of alarm.
What they were listening to was the virtual
announcement that the Treaty of Amiens was
at an end.

The immediate result of the rupture with
England was of a gay rather than a gloomy
character for Josephine. Napoleon decided to
take her with him on a tour through Belgium,
after she had paid an unusually short visit to
Plombières. A letter written from Plombières
to Hortense at Malmaison shows her in low
spirits at their separation.

" I feel that I was not born for so much
greatness," she says, " and that I should be
more happy in retirement, surrounded by the
objects of my affection. I know you, my dear
daughter, and am sure that you, while you make
the happiness of my life, share also all my cares.
Eugène should be with you now. This idea
consoles me. I know well enough your attachment to Bonaparte to be convinced that you
give him your loyal companionship. You owe
him, on many grounds, friendship and gratitude.

. . . Send me news often.   Take good care of my grandchild."

Whatever sentiments this letter conveys, it shows no jealousy of Hortense's relations to Napoleon, nor anything but love for Hortense and her baby.

Josephine returned to Paris before the Belgium tour, and it was on June 24 that she set out with Napoleon from Saint-Cloud for Amiens, the coast ports, and Lille.   From the last-named town she wrote on July 9 another of her affectionate letters to her daughter, part of which deserves quotation :

"I have been meaning, my dear Hortense, to get your brother and my ladies to write to you to give you news of Bonaparte and myself. Since my departure from Paris I have been constantly employed in listening to compliments. You know me, and can judge from this how much I should prefer a quieter life.   Happily the society of my ladies compensates me for the bustling life which I lead.   All my mornings, and often my evenings, are passed in receiving people.   I have now to go to a ball.   This pleasure would have been very agreeable to me if I could have shared it with you or at least seen you enjoy it. The hardship which my heart feels most is that which separates me from my dear Hortense and from my grandson, whom I love almost as much as I love his mamma."

The party passed through Ostend and Bruges to Ghent, where the departmental prefect overwhelmed Josephine with more compliments. " At Ghent," he told her, " they were aware of the empire over hearts which her benevolence exercised. When that virtue of benevolence was accompanied by the irresistible charms of grace, intelligence, and talent, it was all-powerful. So at Ghent everything was subject to her sway." At Antwerp, Malines, and Brussels similar eulogies awaited her. Napoleon was travelling through Beligum in Royal state, attended by diplomatists, ministers, and generals, and even by a Papal Legate, Cardinal Caprara ; and Josephine received the attentions due to a queen. At Brussels a strange scene occurred. High Mass was to be said at the cathedral of Sainte-Gudule, and the clergy had prepared to receive Napoleon at the door and lead him in procession to a throne set up near the altar. But Napoleon, always attentive to historic precedents, was aware that Charlemagne had entered the cathedral by a side door, which bore his name in consequence. Accordingly he told Josephine to take her place with the Second Consul in the gallery, while he entered by Charlemagne's door and seated himself on the throne before the expectant clergy knew that he was in the building.

After Brussels, visits were paid to Liége and Maestricht, and on August 12 Napoleon and Josephine returned to Saint-Cloud, having seen eighty towns in forty-eight days; certainly the busiest forty-eight days in the history of their life together.

The war which had been in progress with England since May made little difference to Josephine except in so far as it absorbed the First Consul, and life went on much as before. So did her struggle with her husband's family. Another member of that family had lately re-appeared to take up the contest after an absence of more than a year. Paulette had gone out most unwillingly to San Domingo at the end of 1801, accompanying her brave young husband Leclerc, the "right hand" of Napoleon, as he himself called him. In January 1803 she returned

MARIE PAULINE, PRINCESS BORGHESE.
From the painting by Lefèvre in the Museum at Versailles.

p. 330.

to France, carrying her husband's heart in an
urn [1] and having cut off all her hair to leave in
his coffin. Napoleon, fond though he was of
Paulette, had remarked : " Oh, she knows her
hair will grow all the better for being cut ! "
He read his sister aright. The inconsolable
widow in the June after her return met at
Joseph's house at Mortefontaine the Roman
Prince Camillo Borghese. This handsome and
elegant young man, who had compromised
himself at home a few years before by espousing
French revolutionary ideas and had publicly
burnt the escutcheon of his rich and noble
family, had rehabilitated himself when he
became head of the family. Introduced to
Joseph Bonaparte by his friend Angiolini, he
had been invited to Mortefontaine. Although
he was ill-educated and singularly devoid of
talent, he made an immediate conquest of
Mme. Leclerc. In her letter from Lille, part

---

[1] On the urn she had inscribed the words : " Paulette
Bonaparte, married to General Leclerc 20 *prairial an V.*, has
enclosed in this urn her love, together with the heart of her
husband, whose dangers and glory she shared." We are reminded of her words to Fréron five years earlier : " I swear,
dear Stanislas, never to love any one but you." And of those
to her lover Forbin in 1807 : " *Addio, caro, sempre caro amico,
amante caro, si ti amo ti amaro sempre.*"

of which is quoted above, Josephine wrote to
Hortense :

" Doubtless you know that Mme. Leclerc is
marrying. She weds Prince Borghese. She
wrote two days ago to Bonaparte to tell him
that she desired him for her husband and that
she felt she would be very happy with him.
She asks Bonaparte to allow Prince Borghese
to write to him to ask for her hand. It seems
that Joseph and M. Angelini [*sic*] made this
marriage. In case the family may not have
spoken to you of it, say nothing about it."

On receiving the Prince's letter, Napoleon
offered no objection to the marriage, but referred
him to Joseph as the head of the family. In such
a matter he preferred to recognise his brother's
seniority, which otherwise counted so little.
Borghese obtained Joseph's consent and at the
end of August was secretly married to Paulette
at Mortefontaine, in the presence of Joseph,
Lucien, and Angiolini. The reason for secrecy
was this : Although Napoleon was willing to
leave the question of their sister's re-marriage
to the natural head of the family, he could not
himself, as head of the State, countenance the
breach of the lately restored *Usages* relating to

mourning, which prescribed a period of one year and six weeks for a husband. Leclerc had only been dead nine months, so that Paulette's violation of the law was scandalous. Napoleon refused to be present at the public civil marriage in November and left for Boulogne without seeing his sister. He had an additional reason for ill-temper, for on October 26 Lucien had been civilly married to the widow Alexandrine Jouberthou or Jouberton, by whom he had already a son. Napoleon called on him immediately to put the woman away, and failing to persuade him to do so, banished him from France in the following spring.

Some of her enemies among the Bonapartes, therefore, were rendering it impossible for them to do harm to Josephine, by themselves forfeiting their powerful brother's regard—Lucien almost permanently, and Paulette for many months. Lucien's removal was undoubtedly an advantage to Josephine, although she had not contributed in any way to his present disgrace, and indeed appears after this to have tried to soften Napoleon's heart toward him. Paulette she had less reason to fear, for her very petulance rendered her animosity comparatively harmless.

Josephine received the newly married Princess at the Tuileries soon after the civil ceremony and was able to inflict a signal defeat to her pretensions by an exercise of that tact which enabled her on so many occasions to be pleasant, but also on a few put it in her power to be unpleasant without leaving her adversary any ground for complaint.

The affair is amusingly described by the Duchesse d'Abrantès, who was an interested spectator. Paulette was to be formally presented to her sister-in-law in her new name and with her new husband. Although it was a November evening, Josephine proceeded to array herself in a white Indian muslin robe, with short sleeves, decorated with a few gold lion-head brooches, while a golden network held up the hair piled on the top of her head. The First Consul, passing her dress under review as usual, exclaimed as he kissed her shoulder : " Josephine, I shall be jealous. You have some scheme on. Why are you so beautiful to-day ? " " I know that you like me in white, and I have put on a white dress. That is all." " Well, if it is to please me, you have succeeded "—and he kissed her again. Josephine awaited her sister-in-law in the large saloon of Saint-Cloud, upholstered in blue, which made an admirable setting to her white muslin dress. Suddenly the doors of the saloon were thrown open and the usher announced " Monseigneur the Prince and Madame the Princess Borghese." Pauline entered in a light green velvet robe, decorated with pearls, emeralds, and diamonds, and with an emerald and diamond tiara on her head. Josephine, assuming royal airs, allowed her to come nearly the length of the room to greet her. Pauline turned to Mme. Junot a few minutes later and said : " My sister-in-law thought to be disagreeable to me in making me come all the way across the room, but she has charmed me. My train would not have been displayed if she had come to meet me, while now it has been admired in its entirety." Suddenly a thought struck her. She turned again to Mme. Junot and said in a desperate whisper : " Good heavens, I have put on a green dress to sit in a blue chair ! " Horror-struck, she rose as soon as she could and bade farewell to Josephine, who smilingly kissed her. Josephine had not designed the situation so humiliating to the *belle des belles,* but at least she had taken advantage of the opening which Fate had offered to her, and the dazzling victory for which Pauline had no doubt looked had been won by Josephine.

The year 1803, which in its middle months seemed to threaten grave dangers to Josephine and almost to promise her enemies the victory for which they prayed, closed with her position rather strengthened and with her enemies disconcerted. It might be that she had reason for doubting, as she did, the faithfulness of her husband to his marriage vow, but, if he allowed himself to stray occasionally, he seemed more than ever determined to prove to her that she was to him the only wife whom he desired and that it was with her that he meant to share the honours which he was confident would be his.

END OF VOL. I.

Printed by Hazell, Watson & Viney, Ld., London and Aylesbury, England.